D0710173

# Survival Kit
## for Marriage

Learning to love through whatever life brings

*Carolyn Shealy Self and William L. Self*

Ministerial Association
General Conference of Seventh-day Adventists

# Introduction

This book began as Sunday School curriculum for a department designed for newlyweds and newly re-weds. The purpose is to help our young couples realistically face married life, learning to understand and love through whatever circumstances may occur.

We use this as a "rollover" seminar, closing the enrollment after the second week and holding the prospects for the next session. They are funneled into their usual departments and classes, and when it is time to start a new group they are transferred temporarily to us. Our newlywed and rewed department is a temporary (four months) seminar. The participants are "on loan" to us from the overall Sunday School and, even though we are very active socially in order to become a cohesive group, they are still tied to their classes.

We also use this material for marriage enrichment retreats, seminars, etc. It is really better to have people who have been married for some time and are more aware of problem areas than newlyweds who are still starry-eyed.

We are very grateful for and happy with the responses to the classes and seminars. We have been "in business" a year and have "graduated" about seventy-five couples. There is no way of knowing what the results will be, but we do know that through better communication several couples have been able to get through some rough waters and realize a deeper and more mature relationship.

This material can also be used with one couple only. Bill and I did the work sheets ourselves as we wrote the material. We did a lot of discussing and faced some shadowy areas in our own relationship. So it has been rewarding for us in many ways. It has also been a lot of fun and made us appreciate each other more than ever.

—Carolyn Self

# Ten Commandments for the Christian Home

1. Thou shalt love the Lord thy God with all thy mind, heart, and soul and honor him in thy home.
2. Thou shalt love each other as you love God—also, respect and like each other.
3. Thou shalt understand that marriage is sacred and is to be nurtured, cultivated, and enjoyed.
4. Thou shalt declare thine independence from thy parents and grandparents and live independently from them.
5. Thou shalt not starve thy children spiritually.
6. Thou shalt love thy children enough to turn them loose when they are of age.
7. Thou shalt set a good example for thy children in worship and Christian morality.
8. Thou shalt realize that marriage is a partnership—each giving and receiving.
9. Thou shalt manage thy money wisely and support the household of faith.
10. Thou shalt provide an atmosphere of Christian culture and values.

# Contents

# 1. The Meaning of Marriage
## (Setting Priorities)

*Bible Passages:*  Ephesians 4:15-16; Philippians 1:9-11;
Colossians 1:9-12; 1 Corinthians 13

*T*he *New York Times Magazine* recently featured an
article about the demise of suburbia. One of the
obvious but still shocking causes of the failure of
suburbia to be the idealistic dream lifestyle we were promised
has been divorce. In 1978 alone there were one million
divorces in the United States. (There were two million
marriages in 1978.) The nuclear family consisting of the
breadwinning father, homemaking mother, and 3.1 children,
all cozy and happy, is getting more and more difficult to find.
When we hear of another divorce we are always asking,
"Why?" "What is happening to marriage?" And we wonder,
"Will it happen to me?"

We need to take a realistic look at what marriage really is.
Marriage is a union of two individuals. Each comes with his
own ideas, attitudes, and ways of doing things and handling
problems. Suddenly he has to learn to live with the other's
ideas, attitudes, and ways of doing things and handling problems. How well the marriage works depends on how well a
person understands himself and how well he can tolerate and
accept the differences of his mate. Someone has said, "All
marriages are happy. It's the living together afterward that
causes the trouble." We are prone to be very impatient when
love and marriage do not solve all of life's previous problems.
Romantic love is not worth anything if it is not well grounded
in reality.

Marriage is overglamorized in the media and we naturally

expect more than any one human can possibly deliver. Husband expects perfection in every area, total cooperation, and understanding; wife expects fulfillment on every level. After all, the advertisements show only gleaming silverware, sparkling crystal, romantic candlelight, clean and cute babies. They never show a sink of dirty, chipped dishes, an unshaven husband, disheveled wife, or a crying, spitting baby with dirty diapers.

Reality is sometimes not only a shock, but also a surprise. Nobody likes surprises like these: he comes home tired and irritable; she is not always sexually responsive; someone has to take out the garbage and clean the bathtub; money will only stretch so far and you thought Daddy was going to provide the extras forever; she's a night person, he's a day person, etc.

We all expect some magic in every place—jobs, home, vacation, children, marriage. We all want the ideal, the perfect in everything. We need to learn that when a good thing happens, when a good relationship develops, it is the result of working creatively with realities, one at a time. A fantasy concept of marriage on the part of either husband or wife needs fast help from a competent counselor. Never hesitate to seek help. It will be a growing experience for both husband and wife.

Giving up "fantasy" or "magical" notions about marriage does not mean you lose the beauty and mystery of this most intimate relationship. It does mean that you can realistically approach each other without having to forever wear a mask or hide a part of yourself. It frees the couple to express, without fear of being misunderstood, their innermost feelings and longings. You can dream together, but also realistically plan together.

Your marriage is not soundly built until married love has taken the place of romantic illusions. Most of married love develops after marriage. This means that even sturdy, married love requires attention to remain healthy. From the very beginning you need to creatively nurture your relationship.

Little things do mean a lot. Bill and I are given to loving greetings and farewells and affectionate glances in a crowd. We are interested in each other's activities and have lots of things we enjoy doing together. Continual nurturing must take place, however you accomplish it. Marriage is potentially the most totally intimate human relationship. It is a beautiful and delicate mystery that is never completely solved; there is always more to discover.

Not only is marriage exciting and mysterious; it is also a frightening step. It is really a "leap into God's arms." Marriage has been compared to a man and woman dancing together on a high tightrope. All have at least one fall; some break their necks when they fall; but if the husband and the wife both have faith and commitment, they fall into the net God spreads out to catch them. There they roll into each other's arms and then they can climb back onto the tightrope again.

A healthy marriage needs to have goals and priorities. There need to be overall, lifetime goals for your lives together, individual goals, and short-term pegs along the way. I don't mean high-sounding goals like these:

**Wife:** "I will make our home a calm, quiet haven of rest; it will be well organized and run smoothly."

**Husband:** "I will provide my family with all the things they need to be happy; my wife can always depend on me for all her needs."

**Wife:** "I know my husband isn't perfect; he drinks too much sometimes and he doesn't always follow through on commitments, but I love him so much and I'll make him so satisfied and happy that he will change."

**Husband:** "We will buy a house in two years, start our family in five years, and go to Europe in about three years. We will be happy."

**Husband and Wife:** "Our goal is to have a successful marriage: a nice home in a nice neighborhood, two cars, intelligent, well-behaved children (a boy first, then a girl), and an ego-satisfying job, total sexual fulfillment every time, no sickness, and no conflict."

These may sound farfetched to you, but they are samples of some ideas that people have about life.

Priorities in any part of life have to be reexamined and readjusted frequently. Now is a good time for you both, individually and as a couple, to do this. Goals play a large part in the patterns we cut out for daily living. Perhaps a good way to identify your priorities will be to state the goals for your life. In order to keep this within the realm of possibility, let's begin with this week. Be thinking of some areas of your marriage that you'd like to change or improve. Perhaps you're getting into a rut or maybe you're having trouble separating your business cares from your home responsibilities. This applies to both husband and wife. One or both may be working outside the home and the frustration experienced at work is easily transferred from that location to home and from co-workers to spouse. You may want to change this pattern. How can you actively work on this?

One couple I know got into an argument nearly every evening after he came home from the office and before dinner. She had gotten into the habit of greeting him with a recitation of all the woes, both great and small, of the day. He had no time to shed the troubles he had accumulated before she hung more on him. He became more and more withdrawn and she resented this feeling of isolation. This situation could be resolved by allowing each one a little space. Let him have some time to shed the office—a glass of juice or a cup of coffee in a quiet spot, with nothing but pleasant conversation or no conversation and no children for even ten or fifteen minutes, will work wonders for the relationship.

One of the most beautiful women I know, Mrs. Baker James Cauthen, in talking about how Dr. Cauthen had been able to literally carry the world in his heart and deal with the day-to-day "nitty gritty," said: "We agreed early that he would not have to rehash his day's work when he came home. I have found my fulfillment in many areas of service and, of course, I'm always ready to listen when he needs me to be a sounding board." This dear couple has been through all the traumas that a long, useful life can bring and are living proof that two people whose commitment is to God and each other can come through it all with grace and dignity. This commitment has been the overall goal in their lives. As the years have gone by, they have examined and adjusted the daily and weekly priorities that are in keeping with their lifetime goals.

Sometimes I hear a remark like: "Jane and Bob have an ideal marriage." Chances are that while Jane and Bob may have a good relationship and life, they also encounter the thorns and booby traps common to human relationships. We should never succumb to the temptation to pattern our lives after others' because what is ideal to one couple may be intolerable to another.

Marriage can be happy, satisfying, successful, and rewarding. It is not a static state of perfection; it must always be a moving, alive relationship, adjusting and changing to accommodate all the situations of life. Did anyone say to you when you married, "Now you can settle down"? They were saying, "Now you're grown up. Now that you are an adult, nothing will change anymore." Nothing should be further from the truth. This would be like saying to a person who has just become a Christian, "Now you're saved; that's all you have to do." The Christian life is to be one of dynamic growth. The New Testament is growth-oriented, and the inspired writers often rebuke Christians for not continuing to grow.

Marriage and families should also experience growth as we move through the changing cycles of life. This cannot be automatic or always upward. Life is a constant "becoming." Then we have to ask, "Becoming what? Where am I going? Where are we going?" Continued growth creates vitality, excitement, feelings of accomplishment, and the ability to cope with crises in one's marriage. There are peaks and valleys in any relationship, and family life is no exception.

## Work Space

*For Group Discussion:*
What were your concepts about marriage prior to the fact?
Were they daydreams or illusions?
Can you cope with this and face reality?

1.  What do you want for your marriage?

    a.

    b.

2.  Married love requires attention to remain healthy. How will you nurture your marriage?

    a.

    b.

3.  Together, decide on some reasonable goals for your marriage. Write them down.

4.  Based on the goals you have set, what are the priorities necessary to reach these? Beginning today, our priorities are:

    a.

    b.

    c.

# 2. *Understand Yourself*
## (Self-Esteem)

*Bible Passages:*          Psalms 139; 8:4-6; Genesis 1:27, 31;
                          5:1-2; Isaiah 45:3-4; Matthew 6:25-34;
                          Exodus 33:17; Luke 12:6-7

Always daughter, wife, mother—never just me, myself.
Always son, husband, father—never just me, myself.

God paid us his highest compliment by created us in his own image. "Male and female he created them, and he blessed them and named them Man when they were created" (Gen. 5:2, RSV). The word for *man* here is the generic term for all mankind. The first question we have to settle is "Who am I?" The nature of our personhood is vital in its importance to Christian marriage. Eric Fromm has said that love is possible only if two people communicate with each other from the very center of their existence. This makes it necessary for each one to experience himself from the center of his being.

Some theologians maintain that the essential nature of male or female in us is the reflection of God's image in us. The equality of personhood is evident in the creation account. Each person, male or female, has infinite worth in God's eyes. Human sexuality seems to have become complicated recently; but when the delivering doctor says, "It's a boy!" or "It's a girl!" almost everyone has a strong appreciation for being male or female. Each person, in his very core of acceptance of himself as a unique individual has a definite sense of being male or female.

It is understood from our studies in psychology that male or female is the gender identity of a person. Masculine or feminine behavior is determined by the accepted definitions of what our culture decrees is proper. When we can accept and be happy with our own sexuality, we will be what God intends for us to be, not what our culture "roles" us to be.

Have you ever had to put down on paper the highlights of your life? The really big events are usually easy to recall; even the facts are pretty well engraved and focused in the memory bank. It is important to have the occasion to probe your memory, to put the pieces of your background in proper perspective. You have to set the stage and remember where you've been to understand who you are now at this moment. Every twenty-four-hour period brings a change in each person because of the people who touched your life and the situations and events that occurred. Where one is born, the type of family life, schooling, friends, church, etc., all add up to making you who you are today.

As you recall these events, notice how what you're really recalling is not necessarily the bare facts, but their appearance—the way you saw and felt them. We can never banish all illusion from facts because all that we have seen and felt, images and sensations, remain somewhat distorted in our memories. What matters is not so much the historical facts, but the *way in which we see and feel them*.

Being open and honest with yourself cannot be stressed enough in this growth study. Trying to fool yourself now will only add to the complications of the future. This doesn't in any way mean to dwell continually on the past and on unpleasant events. It does mean that now is the time to hold them up, look at them realistically, and then put them in proper perspective. So often people are prone to magnify something and make it an obstacle that seems insurmountable. If you discover something of this nature in your background, begin now to pray about it and ask our heavenly Father to help you put it in its proper place. Learn to receive his help in dealing with problems. The Scripture (particularly

Ps. 139) affirms our individual importance to God.

The Bible talks of four kinds of love: (1) God's love for us; (2) our love for God; (3) our love for our fellowman; (4) our love for ourselves. If any one of these gets distorted, the whole love process is deficient in experience. For example, if one doesn't understand God's love, he cannot love himself. And if he cannot love himself, he cannot love his fellowman.

We must value ourselves enough to choose the very best for ourselves. If you don't think you're worth the best, who will? All you have to do is read the Scripture to see that this is God's plan (Joseph: Gen. 39:8-10; Rom. 12:1-3). A person must do good for himself in order to fulfill God's purpose in his life.

You have probably learned by now that you really cannot motivate someone on a long-term basis by saying: "Do it for Mother, or Daddy, or even for God." One has to do it for himself and in that way learn to become what God intends him to be. It does matter what you do to yourself. It is a reflection of what you think of yourself and of God, your Creator.

One definition of love is said this way: "It is the respect, recognition, consideration, and care for other persons." Self-neglect, self-criticism, and self-destruction are symptomatic of serious psychological problems. "Putting yourself down" does not mean that you are "super holy." It really means that you are sick and can't love anyone, including God, in a healthy way. Shakespeare said that self-love is not as vile a sin as self-neglecting.

There is not another you! You are unique and precious to God. The word *precious* is very descriptive of our relationship to the heavenly Father. Even if all your earthly family and friends are destroyed by some disaster, the heavenly Father loves you more than any human ever can. He knows you and loves you and values you with all your humanity. Precious—that's what you are. God knows how many hairs are on our heads, but best of all he knows our names.

A mutually loving relationship is a constantly growing,

changing, challenging experience for both parties. The only way a mature love can come about and be nurtured is for each partner to know himself and to be aware of his own needs, feelings, and experiences. Jesus said to love your neighbor as yourself. You need to know who you are underneath the mask and clothes and learn not to ignore yourself.

There is a big difference in understanding and accepting yourself and in being selfish. You need to respect your own capacities and ideas, not to the point of preoccupation, but to the point of becoming the best "you" possible.

The state of love exists when the satisfaction or security of another person becomes as significant to you as your own satisfaction or security. Marriage will not make you an instant angel or magically end all your problems. The same is true for your partner. Learn to view yourself and others realistically. The good news of God is that he appreciates us. We need to give this, in turn, to others. If we are living in Christ we will allow love to go out from us to others. So being able to appreciate yourself and others is the first step in being able to understand your mate.

There are some questions that will help you understand yourself and your mate better. On the work sheet complete section 4; and when you have completed the questions, compare them with your mate's. Your answers may give some clues to each other as to why you each react as you do.

If you have been married before, you will have to realize that your former spouse is also now a part of your background and a very real part of what you are bringing to this relationship. You must not "put on" your mate the same qualities your former partner possessed. Don't expect anything to be like your former marriage.

You will have to cope with extended families on both sides, plus the ever-present responsibility of children from the former union. Be aware that even the most adorable children are jealous creatures and can undermine the most solid relationship. Read and mark in your Bible Ephesians 4:31-32.

All of these and many more come together to make you

what you are. They definitely affect the way you relate to your spouse. Also, in order for you to understand yourself and appreciate your mate, it is necessary for you to really acknowledge that each person has certain basic rights as an individual. Complete section 5 on the work sheet.

Being married does not mean that you stop being you. You are a whole person yourself—not a half person. Marriage is not two halves coming together to make one viable unit, but two whole people coming together.

Many couples, after the first excitement of being married, fall into living together but keeping themselves hidden from each other. During the courtship and engagement period, a couple may feel very close; they can almost read each other's minds, only to find out five to ten years into the marriage (if not much sooner) that they are not as much alike as they thought. Each person needs to become comfortable with his own sexuality. Being happy in our gender identity enables us to adapt old roles and adopt new roles in fulfilling our under-standing of what it means to be male or female.

One of the most common findings in psychological research is that there is a difference in performance between men and women. In this day of women's liberation, these facts have come under scrutiny again. The facts are that women excel at certain tasks; men excel at others. Women show one perceptual pattern, men another. For years psychologists have maintained that sex differences are due to learning and not biology. In the light of new interest in the matter, researchers are taking a new look at the situation and are coming up with some interesting and different conclu-sions.

Researchers acknowledge that many of our sexual differ-ences reflect social influences, but they now say that the neurological constitutions of men and women lead them to think and behave in different ways. This is based on evidence that women's brains are organized differently from men's for certain tasks and functions. This has nothing to do with overall size or the proportions of parts of the human brain.

Sex hormones have also been given a lot of credit for the difference in males and females. Some speculate that male and female hormones start the process by acting on different parts of the brain and thus producing different behavior. What really matters in all of this is that we individually know who we are and enjoy being male or female, as the case may be.

Male and female complement each other through their differences. Paul Tournier talks about some of these differences in hopes that both sexes will become sensitive to the needs and expressions of each other.

**A woman thinks in terms of people more than ideas.** Men think in theories and the abstract; their thoughts are often detached and unrelated to the immediate situation at hand. For example, a woman seeing a hungry child may immediately make specific preparation to put food in his mouth. A man seeing a hungry child may theorize about a system of aid that could help all hungry children.

**Women are interested in detail more than general ideas.** A woman enjoys knowing exactly what someone was wearing, what was said word for word, etc. Men relate more to general ideas—an outline, a sketch of the situation. Both are important because general ideas are no more than empty theory without concrete and personal details.

**Speech is used differently by men and women.** Men use speech for communicating information and ideas. Women speak to express feelings and emotions. Women sometimes discharge emotional tension which is built up over an experience by telling it not once, but over and over. A women also wants to hear words of love even if she already knows she is loved. Men often do not see the need to say "I love you" after they've said it once or twice, but women need to hear it. Men sometimes express feelings in other ways, like doing something he knows she wants done or buying a gift; men often express feeling with a caress, a look, or even a grunt.

**Career and vocation may well be a misunderstood area.** Women who have exciting careers can understand and have somewhat the same feeling that some men do about their career or profession. If a person has a calling (male or female), the career is more than just a way to earn a living; it is part of the person. She married the person, not his calling. But what a person does all day does seem to become an integral part of him. They then begin to live in two different worlds and each feels shut out from the other. Paul Tournier suggests that a husband and wife should be vitally interested in what interests each other and try to understand why it is interesting.

**Love expressed in sexual intercourse is quite differently experienced and desired by male and female.** Masculine love expressed in sexual experience is often impulsive and of short duration. Feminine love expresses itself more tenderly and continually. This difference is not always present, but occasionally it can lead the woman to have complete disgust for the experience and she may feel that her husband doesn't love her, only wants her. It is important for both husband and wife to understand these differences and for both to make an effort to remember that ideally the sexual experience is a part of the total picture of mutual understanding and communication between the two.

These are but a few of the differences between the sexes. However, it is important to remember that there are not only differences in the sexes, but also in people in general. There are no two women alike and no two men alike. Each of us is truly a marvel of God's creation.

## Work Space

1.  Remember the big events and important people in your life. Jot down key words or phrases for these so that you can go back later and consider the effect they had on you.
    a.

    b.

    c.

    d.

2.  Read again Psalm 139. Underline verses 13-16. Let these words sink into your mind and heart, and remember them when you feel insecure and forgotten.

3.  Think about yourself honestly and answer these questions:
    a.  What do I like about myself?
    b.  What do I not like about myself?
    c.  What am I really like?
    d.  Can I be alone, but not lonely?
    e.  Can I manage my money and living conditions (before marriage)? Am I competent to understand and manage the family finances?
    f.  Do people listen to me and hear what I am saying? Do I feel good about what I say, or do I feel foolish?
    g.  Do I spend a lot of time feeling guilty and/or "put upon"?
    h.  Am I basically afraid of people, situations, of being wrong, or myself, etc.?
    i.  Do I feel that I am a worthwhile person in myself, or do I feel that I need to be needed in order to justify my existence?

    j.   Can I relax and play, or do I have to make every minute count?

    k.   Am I a jealous person?

    l.   Do I like being a woman/a man?

    m.   Do I feel responsible for making my mate happy? Is he/she responsible for making me happy?

4.  There are many reasons behind the way you react and respond to each other. Think about your background. These questions will stimulate your understanding of yourself and your mate:

    1.   Can you think of a word or phrase that would describe your parents?

    2.   Were they religious? Legalistic? Permissive?

    3.   Were you happy as a child (generally speaking)? As an adolescent?

    4.   Were you reared in a one-parent family? If yes, which parent?

    5.   Do you have siblings?

    6.   Was there much sickness in your home?

    7.   Do you want to be like your mother/father? If yes, why? If not, why?

    8.   Did you grow up in the church?

    9.   Are you from a small town? Large city? Rural background?

    10.  Did you go to college?

    11.  Have you had a work experience?

    12.  How was anger handled in your home?

    Now compare your answers with your mate.

5.  List five basic rights you feel you can claim as an individual. (Example: space for myself—within limits, not to point of worry for mate).

    1.

    2.

3.

4.

5.

Now share these with your mate. When they are written down, do they seem reasonable? Discuss how you can resolve any major differences; try to understand and be ready to compromise. Learning to compromise can be very creative.

6. Can you allow each other space to move and grow and then come together appreciating the resourcefulness and creative ability of each other?

# 3. *Understand Each Other*
## (Relating as Husband and Wife)

*Bible Passages:*     Ephesians 5:21 to 6:4; Matthew 20:25-28; Colossians 3:18-19; Titus 2:4-5; 1 Peter 3:7; Romans 14:7-12; Galatians 5:16-25; 6:7-8

We have been talking about self-esteem and the importance of knowing deep inside that "I" am important; "I" am accepted for just being me. Understanding one's own personhood is really basic to all of our relationships. Now we need to talk about the way we relate as husband and wife. We must realize that we relate to a whole person who is a product of his environment, genetic heritage, and tradition as handed down in his family and community. Also, we must never forget that we are not static but living, ever changing, and we have to fit the pieces together as they are given to us. Each person usually presents to the world an image that he wishes to hide behind. The image one projects at church may be very different from the image he becomes at work, and both of these may be very different from what he becomes at home.

A couple having problems talked to a counselor. The husband was very critical of his wife, and she had a list of grievances also. I wonder what he would have said of her when they were dating. She probably has changed, but not as much as he thinks. He had seen her with the eyes of love and had formed an idealized image of her. It was the image he loved, believing it to be the reality. The image he now repels and condemns is not his wife any more than the idealized image was. They need to strip away the images they have created for each other and really allow themselves to know and be known by the other. Only through communion can we get behind the images and know the person.

I have used *image* almost interchangeably with the term *role*. *Position* in the setting is also a descriptive word for this purpose. We are asked, "What is your position in your company?" In other words, "What role do you play when you are at your job?" We do have a position to fill, a role to play in every area of life. The world of work and the world of the family are usually the two that occupy most of our time, but these overlap and have a lot to do with how we fill any other roles, such as at church and socially.

The term *role* is used to refer to (1) a set of expectations concerning what a person in a given position must, must not, or may do, and (2) the actual behavior of the person who occupies the position. The idea is that anyone occupying a position and filling a role behaves similarly to anyone else who would be in that position.

Example (a): A receptionist in any office is expected to perform certain tasks in an acceptable way; to be polite, pleasant, but not overly friendly; to give and receive information; to look presentable as would be appropriate for the firm.

Example (b): The president of a bank is expected to act, talk, and look like an executive who can be trusted; outbursts of profanity or a whining, pitiful voice are not appropriate for this position.

Role concepts have at least three major uses: (1) they help us understand similarities in the behavior of different people in the same positions or situations; (2) they help explain why a person behaves differently as he moves from one position in society to another (for example, from secretary at office to hostess at home; from managing people on a large scale at work to cutting the grass at home); (3) they help in dealing with recurrent patterns of interaction between two or more people who occupy adjacent positions in the social network (for example, interaction among bride, groom, and minister;

doctor, patient, and nurse).

Fulfilling a social role does not eliminate all individuality. Different people will fulfill the role in different ways because the prescription for filling the role is not always precise. There are always certain areas that are mandatory, but large areas of "filling in the blanks" exist (for example, parents are expected to feed and care for their children, but there is great latitude in how you do it). People also vary in their perceptions of a role (for example, President Lyndon Johnson horrified people by driving his Lincoln about at breakneck speeds, disregarding the fact that his position required more caution concerning physical risk).

Fulfilling a role makes it difficult to "be ourselves." We all yearn for this and are afraid we'll forget what we'd be like if we were allowed to "be ourselves." Bill and I had some very serious discussions during our dating days. In fact, I felt that I could not fill the role of a minister's wife, so we broke up for five or six months. I knew I loved Bill, but I tried really hard to deny it, rather than face the difficulties I knew would come with the marriage. All the ministers' wives I had known filled the expected role beautifully (to public view anyway), and I just couldn't. I've never been a good game player. After much prayer, soul searching, and discussion, Bill and I got back together with the understanding that I could be me. The first four years we were married, we spent finishing college and seminary with no regular pastor-church responsibilities and I was spared that which I feared most. Then came the first church and first child and I felt swallowed up. Everybody in that eastern North Carolina community was an authority on the behavior and attitude of the pastor and his wife, and neither of us fit any of them! What an experience! I almost didn't come out of those years alive, but we both learned a lot. I found out that being Bill's wife was important, but I had to work at being me first and not allow everyone to manipulate my life. You can't believe the pressures people bring to control the preacher's family. You have to develop strength and determination to maintain any individuality. This applies not only to ministers' families, but to anyone who at any time in life is overwhelmed by one person or a group of people. Sometimes you have to fight for your life—and it's worth it!

Sex-typing in our culture is an interesting phenomenon. This is a process by which we define the emotional responses, personality, attitudes, and beliefs appropriate for male and female in our culture. Even books on this subject as current as this year are in impressive agreement as to what our society says constitutes masculine and feminine behavior.

Tradition maintains its formative power in spite of feminist movements. Through the ages men have had the instrumental role: getting things done; taking on tasks that are physically strenuous or dangerous. Men are taught to be independent, aggressive, dominating, and emotionally inhibited in order to carry out male assignments, such as building bridges, sailing ships in rough seas, and "scaling the corporate walls." In turn, women have assumed passive, dependent, expressive roles. They are taught to be warm, indecisive, submissive, and reliant on men. The traditional role for women is centered around taking care of others, nursing, cleaning, cooking, and other related tasks.

A study done recently showed that regardless of sex, marital status, or educational level of the people interviewed, masculine characteristics were valued more highly except when those characteristics were assumed by women. In this case, masculine characteristics were considered to be symptomatic of a problem (poor mental health). This sex-typing limits the alternatives of both men and women. In practicality, the alternatives of women are less desirable.

Does all this "role" business begin at home? It is thought that modeling for boys and girls generally is learned at home. That is, boys identify with fathers and girls identify with mothers. However, this is not the case in more and more instances. In many families the father is away from home during the daylight hours, and often for the business week. Mother is the one who cares for infants and children of both sexes, and they initially identify with her. This is allowed to continue for the daughter; but since it is inappropriate for a son, it will be discouraged. Because of his father's absence much of the time, the boy must piece together a masculine model from observing not only his father but other male models, including neighbors, relatives, and TV heroes.

Sex-typing, or the learning of sex-appropriate behavior, begins during the early months as a mother decreases the amount of physical contact accorded a son but increases the amount accorded a daughter. Elementary school teachers are usually feminine models. Symbolic masculine models are likely to dominate reading materials. During the school years, organizations such as the Boy Scouts and Girl Scouts provide sex-appropriate models and reward sex-appropriate behavior. Sex-typing is further encouraged by conformity pressures exerted by same-sex peers. Sex-typing continues through adolescence.

Changing conditions may result in a greater number of options remaining open for members of both sexes. Technological advancements are rendering inconsequential certain biological differences between the sexes. Female infants, as well as male infants, may now be encouraged to identify with abstract role models rather than with specific individuals. Patterns of reinforcement seem to be changing, as shown by the opening up of occupational opportunities for women. As a result of these factors, both men and women may gain the freedom to choose either the instrumental or the expressive role, depending on inclination or situation. This freedom may lead to new, high levels of psychological well-being.

Most people today know that both husband and wife must play many roles in marriage, but they do not always emotionally accept this. We usually don't even think about it until after the marriage ceremony and the living together begins. Our role expectations come marching forth as soon as a meal is prepared and the garbage can is full.

What is a husband? Men are faced with dilemmas and anxieties. A man must be many things to many people: wage earner, lover, protector, father, good citizen, active church member. He is expected to give time to his family, church, and civic activities and help his wife with household tasks.

Men who have responsible positions are under constant pressure to produce more in order to advance. These pressures cause stress, which is very dangerous. That is why so many young men have heart attacks; and many die as a result.

A husband's primary responsibility is to support the family. This remains the same throughout most of his life. This is his anchor and is an advantage psychologically.

What is a wife? A wife fills many roles in the course of her life. In the first years it seems most important to be a loving wife. Later, her chief job may become mother, or supplementary wage earner, if there is a financial emergency. She may have children to rear, a house to run, and a full-time job; and she may feel open to criticism if she cannot manage all these with equal energy, interest, and ease. If the husband is extremely busy with his work or traveling a great deal, she has to learn to cope with repair people, financial concerns, discipline of children, community responsibilities, keeping the house in repair, and other related activities.

This can be an exciting challenge to some women, but to others it quickly becomes a nightmare. To deal with conflicts and decisions constantly requires a lot of emotional energy and courage because very often there is no previous experience to shed light on the situation. And usually there are no certain answers.

The roles of husband and wife change as a marriage advances from stage to stage; they vary with social patterns and are affected by the cultural background of each spouse.

What kind of marriage do you want? Let's take a look at some of the options. Tradition urges a woman to be an old-fashioned, submissive, obedient, worshipful wife. A woman was taught to do what she was told by her husband, even when she didn't agree with him. In order to keep the peace, she must suppress her feelings of hostility and resentment. Tradition insists that a man be totally responsible for the security (financial and emotional) of his family. He must take charge, issue orders, and make decisions.

Present educational standards urge women and men to have a partnership marriage. This requires knowledge and patient working through situations, with flexibility being the key. This cannot be a type of equal marriage where a score-card is kept (either figuratively or in reality) because it will get to be ridiculous and you'll need a bookkeeping system for that! Partnership marriage makes possible a continuous transfer of authority back and forth between the couple. They are like a team of racing drivers, both taking turns at the wheel. This also allows individual areas of competence to rule in sharing the duties.

Several years ago Bill and I were with a group, driving through the Sinai Desert to Mount Sinai. We were on a bus built especially for desert travel, and all sorts of precautions and preparations had been made for this difficult, rigorous trip. We even had two bus drivers besides our Israeli guide. As we left Mount Sinai, we were traveling as fast as possible over the single lane road in order to be out of the desert and onto the main road before nightfall. We were amazed to see our drivers shift positions, one sliding into the driver's seat as the other slipped out. We never slowed down, swerved to either side, or hit a rock or hole as they did it. Those who weren't watching or were in the rear of the bus never knew what happened. That is what partners in marriage should be able to do with accomplishment. Sometimes one is too tired to be "in charge" or needs help in coping. The relationship should be such that a word or glance will be all that's necessary for the other to step in and smoothly manage until the other is ready to go again. It is a beautiful picture of the ultimate in teamwork. No one is threatened, and both are better for it.

There is a lot of talk today about submissive wives, and some herald a lot of rules and regulations and false doctrines on this matter. Let's put mutual equality and submission in biblical perspective. In this discussion we will follow closely the study of John C. Howell in his excellent book *Equality and Submission in Marriage*. He treats all the Scripture used in a very scholarly and realistic way, interpreting the difficulties we encounter with what many people consider Paul's male chauvinistic attitude. He also removes the club which authoritative men have held over women all these years. What we come out with is a beautiful pattern for relationships which require devotion and constant work on the part of both husband and wife. A good definition for the Christian family is a mutual yieldedness in love, based on the fact that Christ is the Lord of life and home.

Have your Bibles open to Ephesians 5:21 to 6:4 for this study. In verse 33b, "Every husband must love his wife as himself, and every wife must respect her husband" (TEV), Paul was speaking to the Christian family living in a pagan Greek and authoritarian Hebrew culture. It was a difficult time for all people, especially women and slaves.

Read these Scriptures in a modern translation: Ephesians 5:22-24; Colossians 3:18; Titus 2:4-5.

At the time Paul wrote this, the man had legal authority over his wife and she had no choice other than to accept his authority. In Greek culture the women were considered to be permanent minors, always controlled by a male guardian (father, husband, state), and were closely guarded and secluded. In Hebrew culture a female was always under the jurisdiction of a male. She was never her own person, only property to be sold. She would naturally have hostility toward men.

Paul was saying that the Christian woman must have a new attitude toward her Christian husband. She is to voluntarily yield in love to him, based on her own experience of salvation through yielding her life to Christ. She is to accept him as a Christian husband to whom she can truly give herself in love and respect.

The New Testament world was male-dominated in every area. The family was patriarchal with the husband as the head (lord and master). Translating the idea of headship into modern terms, the concept of *responsibility* is acceptable. *Authority is not domination, but responsible headship for the family.* When the husband accepts and acts on his responsibility in Christ, then he is worthy of trust and respect (Eph. 5:33).

Love and respect go hand in hand, but evidently Paul was speaking to a critical problem of that day when he insisted on respect and neglected to mention love to the wife. (Titus 2:4-5 tells older women to teach young wives to love their husbands and children.) A woman had to live under the authority of her husband because the law required it, but she (if she had any intellect and feelings at all) was probably feeling squelched and like a nonperson and could make his life miserable if she so desired. She had many ways (and still does) to "punish" him for her position. Actually, Paul was right to insist on *respect* because that is a very necessary quality if love is to grow through the years. Because most marriages were prearranged in New Testament times, love was not considered a necessary prelude to marriage as it is today. If it happened, that was serendipity in that era. Respect was essential to the relationship, and affectionate love should result from that between Christian spouses.

Now read these verses: Ephesians 5:25-31; Colossians 3:19; 1 Peter 3:7.

Paul gave some reactionary words to husbands of New Testament days. Surely many husbands loved their wives, but more probably used wife and home for convenience. The word for love used here is *agapao,* which means "to esteem and value the object of love to such a degree that one gives his best for that object." As God so loved the world that He gave his only Son to redeem it, so the Christian husband is to so love and value his wife that he voluntarily yields his life into partnership with her in marriage. John C. Howell says, "It is impossible to love one's wife in accord with this biblical description of love without voluntarily surrendering an auto-cratic spirit of domination over her life. Instead, a man is to accept his wife as an *equal partner* in creating a marital rela-tionship which honors that kind of love. The husband's voluntary yieldedness in love fulfills the command to be submissive or subordinate to one another in reverence for Christ." [1]

In Christian marriage, the wife is to be accepted as a person in her own right. The husband is to accept and respect her personhood as equal to his personhood.

A husband should make a habit of loving his wife so that she is sure that he truly loves her and cares for her. She should not need to wonder about this. Ephesians 5:25-27 illustrates the fact that a husband is to pattern his love after the love of Christ for the church. Christ loved the church so deeply that he surrendered his own best interest out of consideration for the best interest of the church. A husband will love his wife to the extent that he considers her best interest first and will give up his own best interest so that hers will be advanced. In this way his authority is expressed in self-giving! To understand more fully this "new" authority that Jesus taught, read Matthew 20:25-28. In Christian love, authority is surrendered and self-giving is required.

In Ephesians 5:28-31 Paul expressed the mutual commitment of marriage. In modern translations this passage speaks for itself in a beautiful way. Also in 1 Corinthians 7:3-5, he described the one-to-one relationship in marriage based on equality of personhood. Again, Paul was probably called a radical for even suggesting that a woman had needs to be met and should rightfully expect her husband to meet them. Just as radical was the idea that the wife has authority over the husband's body! This makes the man and woman equally responsible for meeting the needs of one another and showing proper respect for each other. We know that in New Testament times the men were the sole providers of income, and Paul told the Christian husband to provide and care for his wife adequately.

Complete understanding of another person is impossible,

[1]John C. Howell, *Equality and Submission in Marriage* (Nashville: Broadman Press, 1979), p. 72. Italics were added for emphasis.

but Paul saw the need of understanding in a committed relationship. First Peter 3:7 is translated in various ways, but basically it means, "Live with your wives, trying to understand them in every way; be sensitive to their feelings and needs." He stressed again the equality of women in inheriting the grace of God. She is an equal partner and deserves his respect. One's wife is to be given highest value in his life because of who she is and because she is his joint partner. There is no disgrace in a man yielding himself to the woman he loves and whom he values above all other earthly benefits.

In this area of understanding, we should read again Paul Tournier's beautiful book *To Understand Each Other*. He says that love and understanding are so closely related that we can't know where one ends and the other begins. We all know that when we feel understood, we feel loved. When we are loved, we feel sure of being understood.

There are some very dangerous models for marriage that are being espoused far and wide and creating untold numbers of counseling situations for the solid, "steady in the boat" pastors and counselors. These models being urged on people as the answer to all their problems fall for the most part in the patriarchal or traditional styles. Most of these have rigid role theories and proof-text their way to prove their positions. This takes away the freedom of the believer to be guided by the Holy Spirit in this area of life that dominates all of life. Each one of these self-proclaimed authorities has some good points, but most of their ideas are outweighed by contradictory ideas, if followed to logical conclusions and solutions. The number of books and seminars giving specific instructions and pat answers to all family problems point up the desire of people to achieve instant happiness and acquire peace at any price. Couples are afraid to express their own individuality, and they forget that God made us all different and that what works for one family may be disastrous to another. Many people who are desperately seeking help in a marriage or family situation have ended up in deeper trouble, both emotionally and in the marriage. The psychiatric institution where I worked as a therapist for a time seemed to be the next step for women who desperately needed self-esteem and whose husbands had received further permission to break their spirit. Suicide has seemed the only way out for a few who reached the breaking point.

The problem with such teaching is that so many people want easy 1-2-3 answers to these delicate areas of life instead of thinking, praying, loving, and understanding the other persons. You cannot pull the file card and give an easy, quick answer to these tender situations.

One of the serious theological mistakes of some evangelists is in the umbrella idea of authority. Some say that based on Genesis 3, the husband's salvation provides for the wife's salvation. This is in contradiction to what we believe—that the individual is accountable to God for his actions. We cannot accept Christ's redemption for another person (Rom. 14:7-12; Gal. 5:16-25; 6:7-8).

Several books currently on the market teach submission of women. I cringe at the urging of women to use manipulation to get what they want. This doctrine is basically for extremely immature women who do not want to relate other than in a manipulative way. Some never get beyond this and we know it "takes all kinds."

Work it out for yourselves! As a couple you will need to be open to each other, to communicate your honest feelings about marriage. Remember that this relationship has to grow and change throughout all the years to come. The alternative is the same as not having any more birthdays—death. Your marriage will die. Unfortunately, you may not discover this fact until it begins to stink! Marriage is a process never finished—sometimes bumpy and difficult—hopefully exciting, stimulating, and fun! Your marriage is uniquely yours. It will not be like anybody else's, and you should never try to pattern after what you see and observe of another marriage. It's what you don't see that may scare you! Have fun while growing in this sacred relationship.

### Work Space

1.  What is a wife?

2.  What is a husband?

3.  List adjectives to describe how you feel about your:

**Husband**                          **Wife**
a.                                    a.

b.                                    b.

c.                                    c.

d.                                    d.

4.  When you were a child, what did you want to be when you grew up?

5.  My marriage is like . . . (use descriptive terms such as boss/employee, partners, etc.).

6.  Do you ever envy your spouse? If so, why?

7.  For group discussion—What should you think of a marriage in which the wife went out to work and the husband stayed home?

8.  From your viewpoint, is there a couple who you think has a really good marriage? Who? Why do you think so?

9.  Your marriage will not be like that of any other couple. Your marriage is unique. Never try to make it fit the mold that seems to work for someone else. Marriage is a growing process and should never be finished "till death do you part."

# 4. What Is Communication?

*Bible Passages:*      Proverbs 10:12-14; 12:17-19; 15:1-4,
                       28; 18:13; James 1:19; 5:16; 1
                       Corinthians 13; Luke 12:13-21

*N*ot long ago I heard of a family who used a very cruel form of punishment. When someone in the family (other than the father) was not performing acceptably, communication would be withdrawn from that person. At this particular time, it seems that the wife had not been able to make the teenage children clean their rooms and curb their rebellious attitudes. Father decreed that neither he nor the children would talk to her until she remedied the situation. They did not even acknowledge her on Mother's Day.

Needless to say this is a very sick family, but there are many families who arrive at a communication stalemate without really knowing how it happened.

There is a game which young people used to play at parties that, if prolonged unduly, can be terrifyingly brutal. All the guests agree to act normally toward everyone except for one individual who is not informed. He is ignored, stared through, not responded to. Later the victim is asked to describe his feelings. This game proves the importance of communication as the maintenance for any intimate relationship.

Communication is the means by which relating takes place. Good communicators have the ability to transmit and receive meanings. This is done in many ways. You can tell how deep a relationship is by the number of levels on which communication can take place. You have to care very deeply about a person to be willing to put forth the effort to really communicate.

Communication in marriage is a constant exchange of messages between spouses by speech, letter, telephone, bodily or facial expressions, and many other ways. Everything a person does in relation to another is some kind of message. There is no way not to communicate. We are always communicating, even when we don't wish to or even know it: gestures, roll of the eyes, turn of the back, shrug of the shoulders, tone of voice, or silence. The way one turns toward or away from the other, the raising of an eyebrow, a frown, a half-smile, and the act of reaching out for a hand all convey messages, either intended or otherwise. The closing (or slamming) of a door, the quickness (or slowness) of one's walk, the way one sits, or the avoidance of meeting one's eyes (or holding lingeringly to a tender or understanding look) all speak more than words.

Marriage is a feeling system in which the behavior and attitudes of each has a profound effect on the other. Both negative and positive feelings are transmitted nonverbally as well as verbally. Mislabeled communications pass between spouses frequently. Often the message sent is not the message received.

Verbal communication is very painful for many people. Sometimes one partner is very verbose and will talk a situation to death, while the other partner may have very little or nothing to say. Since it has all been said (or so it seems), the silent one stews inwardly and feels very inadequate to voice any feelings whatsoever. Perhaps this fear turns to apathy; why bother to iron out differences? The passive partner tries to sit out his troubles by eating, sleeping, drinking, watching TV, playing golf or bridge, shopping, etc. This person forgets how to feel and becomes detached, uninvolved, unrelated to the issue. A person who does this must be helped to feel again; one cannot recognize love and affection if he does not also recognize anger and hostility.

Learning to listen is an art in itself. Then being able to read all the signs and respond accordingly is an ongoing process. Communication cannot take place if only one person responds. It is like a telephone call; if the person on the other end doesn't answer there is no way to leave a message. If you keep getting no answer or a busy signal, you will soon quit trying to communicate at all or resort to a letter. Written communication is no substitute for a warm body response, but a letter is necessary to keep the lines open when one is out of town. When one spouse is out of town for more than a day, a phone call is a wonderful communication tool. Much can be communicated by inflections of voice. If you know the person you're talking to, you can tell if he is angry, ill, depressed, happy, trying to hide something, etc. It is important when one is away from family and friends to hear the voice of a loved one. It is soothing and keeps one in touch with reality. Knowing that one is loved and appreciated makes the work worthwhile.

Communication is always a two-way street. The statements a couple make to each other have to be understood against the background of what has happened between them in the past. It is a process of complicated relating, a circular pattern of behaving and responding according to what each has experienced over a period of time.

A communication problem occurs when a message has two or more possible meanings. The listener may interpret the message incorrectly. Sometimes if we are hurt or angry, we may "hear" the wrong thing because of our feelings. Things get very complicated. It is true that the more a couple quarrels, the more likely they will misunderstand each other. Often one spouse will attempt to be witty at the expense of the other. This should be stopped before it becomes a habit. Stop and think how you would feel if the wit were at your expense.

Learning to communicate in mutually affirming ways should be a continuing growth experience in marriage. When you committed yourselves to each other before God, you mutually accepted the responsibility of nurturing each other. The biblical term for consummation of a marriage is "to know." This is a beautiful word to describe the marriage relationship at its best. To this one we can bare our deepest thoughts, desires, dreams, and ambitions and rest assured that we will not be laughed at or scorned.

**There must be ample time set aside for real communication.** A complaint that marriage counselors hear constantly is "He never listens to me" or "What I say goes in one ear and out the other" or "How can I know what he thinks if he won't respond?" You owe it to yourself and to each other to devote some special time each day to listening uninterrupted to each other. Depending on schedules, you can find at least thirty minutes for each other every day. One couple I know are early risers and enjoy a quiet time together over coffee before the children are up. It is a good beginning for the day. For those who can't do that, it is important to at least touch base with each other before leaving home. Perhaps a touch and "I'll be thinking of you today" or "I know you have a hard day ahead; I'll be praying for you" will be a bright spot to remember. At an appropriate time in the evening, a couple might turn off the television and put down the newspaper and talk and listen to each other. Talk about your work, office problems, career frustrations, problem children at school, or whatever your day has encompassed. Take turns and open up honestly; then listen not only to the words spoken but to the in-depth meanings. Perhaps you can pick up on a desperate need. Many times we want closeness but fear the exposure. We may feel that if we really listen, we may hear a criticism or a demand we cannot meet or even be required to change a preconceived notion or opinion. To really listen to another means both giving oneself and being willing to receive the other within oneself. What is really necessary is a *willingness to consider the other's point of view.* It boils down to caring about the other person: caring about his ideas, how he feels, what he thinks, what he is saying. Care enough to listen and internalize what you hear.

**Check out meanings.** This can help both partners improve the way they send messages and also their skills in listening. Sometimes one will send a message that he is not aware of. Ask questions such as: "Is this what you're saying?" or "What I hear you saying is. . . . Is this true?" Be sure you understand what the other feels, means, intends. What you are really saying in this checking-out procedure is: "I really care about you and what you are feeling. I want to hear you correctly."

**Learn to say what you mean.** Listen to yourself and see if you are saying what you really mean. Learn to say what you mean without being abrasive or using an attacking manner. Say "I feel . . ." rather than "You are . . ." or "You always. . . ." If you want something, say so rather than hinting or beating around the bush about it and then being hurt when your spouse doesn't respond "correctly." Playing games this way can be very dangerous to a relationship.

**Become aware of your own and your mate's coded and conflicted messages.** Many times we are totally unaware of the conflicting messages we send. For example: A husband may say loving things and act as if he wants to have a quiet, intimate evening; then the phone rings and a buddy says he has one extra ticket to a ball game. The husband is off, leaving the wife alone to decipher the message. Nagging may be a way of saying that the spouse is not giving what she wants. A wife who talks continuously or interrupts frequently may be asking for attention. Not all coded messages are negative. A gift for no reason at all may be "I love you." There are many couples whose nonverbal communication is on a positive level most of the time; in this way they are continually saying, "I love you."

## Barriers to Communication

Home is where we pin our hopes for being understood. A good communication system in the home is the means by which family life is creative and delightful or a place to shrivel and hurt, a place for growth or neglect, a heaven or hell.

One of the necessary ingredients in a workable marriage is trust. To have faith and confidence in your spouse is absolutely necessary for a relationship that even begins to approach happiness. Probably the biggest barrier to real, open communication between spouses is lack of trust. *Trust* in marriage is different than the usual definition of the word. Trust in marriage is formed on the basis of behavior and information which go on all the time. During times of stress, unclear communication, or confusion, the trust existing between the couple may temporarily diminish; but if handled properly the experience will ultimately strengthen the trust level. Trust is developed over a period of time as a result of experience. If the behavior of each person is generally consistent, each will know he can depend on this. When you can trust your spouse you can relax; then mutual confidence develops. Trust is the result of a flexible, growing relationship that will endure because it can accommodate change. This trust has to be a two-way exchange. It won't work for one to be trusting and trustworthy and the other to be dishonest and deceiving.

Trust brings many rewards to a couple. It automatically brings honesty and open, clear communication. This in turn brings encouragement for spouses to be generous, comforting, and consoling. This is a beautiful gift to give each other.

*Lack of trust* creates great barriers in communication. We can see an example of this in a young couple who came for counseling recently. Jack constantly attacks his wife for spending "so much money." She is trying to be careful and to keep the budget, and she becomes resentful of and hostile to his outbursts. He is actually fearful of losing his job; he feels very insecure at work and is acting out his frustrations by criticizing his wife. If he could be open and truthful about himself and admit his problem, he could receive the comfort and support he is desperately crying for.

If a person can be honest enough to recognize and admit his own weaknesses and finds he can be forgiven, then he can in turn be tolerant and forgiving. Tolerance and generosity are treasured gifts to be given and received.

During courtship we tend to put forth our very best effort

in being kind, attractive, and fun to be with. It is easy to create an image that is impossible to maintain because it isn't natural. It takes a very mature, realistic determination to be truthful and to honestly say to the spouse who assumed you really enjoyed going to the art museum every Saturday: "I really don't enjoy going *every* Saturday. Let's do something else for a change." She may react with surprise, wondering why he never expressed this opinion before. Probably he was afraid that she would think he was not as appreciative of the arts as she assumed he was and didn't want to disappoint her. Many times we set ourselves up as being more than we are; then we have to live with that image. It becomes more and more *difficult to wear the mask at all times*. If they managed to talk freely about this they would probably discover that both had "assumed" the other preferred that activity, when in actuality each one longed for a walk in the woods or a drive in the country.

A young man told me recently of an example in his own life of trying to hide his real feelings because he *feared exposure and hurting his wife's feelings*. It was a little thing, but the little things are only indicative of the larger problems we hide. His bride of several months cooked a delicious roast exactly the way he liked it—just a little pink in the center, nice and juicy. The dinner was delicious and he told her so. The next evening he came home to dinner and she had made hash out of the leftover roast. It was OK but overcooked. She asked if he liked it and he said he did (he didn't want to hurt her feelings). Actually, he had envisioned nice, thick sandwiches from the leftover roast and had his "mouth set" for that. As time went on, more roasts were cooked and served, with the same leftover pattern following. Finally, after seeing his delicious sandwiches take the form of hash one time too many, he told her how he felt about it. She was shocked: "I thought you liked hash. You said you did." He had to tell her that he had just told her that because they hadn't been married long and he was afraid he would hurt her feelings. It is true that we often eat and live hash simply because we are afraid to communicate honestly.

Communication between a couple (and the children also) becomes distorted when *common courtesies are not observed.* When we treat our loved ones disrespectfully or in a demeaning way, we cannot expect the relationship to bloom. Little courtesies and simple good manners go a long way in making life pleasant. We offer friends and even strangers courtesies that we forget to give each other. Can you find yourself in any of these situations? (1) She listens for hours to problems of others, but has no time to listen to him. (2) He complains because dinner isn't to his liking. Would he call a hostess at a dinner party a lousy cook if the roast wasn't prepared the way he liked? (3) She goes to the supermarket neatly dressed and smiles at the people, but she goes to bed with her hair in curlers, cream on her face, and a torn gown, expecting love. (4) He helps other women in and out of cars, carries packages for them, leaving his wife to do the best she can. (5) She wouldn't fly into a rage at a guest who was ten minutes late for dinner, but heaven help her husband who is a few minutes late. (6) He wouldn't expect someone else to be his servant; nor would she expect someone else to be her hatchet man. (7) He leaves his wife at a party, totally forgetting her, so that he can wander and flirt.

Money can become a huge barrier to communication. Sometimes it seems that everything ends up being related to money. Setting up a workable, acceptable budget requires communication, real openness, and calm agreement. It requires a great deal of give-and-take, but most of all *trust in each other.*

Sometimes lack of money can be traced to immature or unrealistic attitudes toward the use of income. If you are having trouble meeting payments and feel yourself being overwhelmed by charge accounts, it is time to learn to work together to develop healthy attitudes about money. This is important because the attitudes a couple develops about handling money will carry over into other areas of marriage. Handling money, even on the level of family finances where only the salary check is involved, can become a nightmare. We work frantically to get more money for very good and ethical reasons. We drive ourselves to a panic and forget to check out the real reason behind our goals. If we had to choose between poverty and wealth, we'd all come down on the side of wealth; but for the moment, we'd like a "good living."

Poverty is something that most of us will never have to face. However, we do come in contact with those who have to deal with poverty as the controlling force in their lives. Children who grow up with the scars of poverty are deeply affected, not only physically, but many times with acute emotional problems.

Guilt and shame are inevitable companions to those who find themselves caught in the trap of this misery. Even if the circumstances are beyond human control, the people (adults and children) feel the oppression also of guilt and shame.

Judgment seems to loom everywhere. It is hard not to say about the poor: "If they would only . . ." or "Look how they waste what they do have" or "It's easier to live on welfare than to work." Middle-class people, without being aware of it, tend to look scornfully, pityingly, or condescendingly on those who are shabbily dressed. This adds the problem of a poor self-image from which children of poverty rarely recover.

Wealth is generally thought of as the solution to all human problems. Many times we let the slender threads that could possibly lead us to wealth slip away almost unnoticed. We have many opportunities that we refuse to acknowledge that could lead to a better financial condition. Wealth, of course, is not the panacea to all the ailments of society. The rich have problems with drug and alcohol abuse, health, family quarrels, divorce, etc., as do the poor. A person who has a great deal of money is always afraid of being used by people. He will always have so-called "friends" who will only see him as a source of money, always a donor to their needs and projects. He may never have to worry about the necessities of life, but he must learn the fine art of managing well what God has given him to control. He must understand himself and his wealth in order not to be totally immobile and unable to function appropriately.

Guilt and shame also haunt the rich and/or middle classes. Many times we play the piety game; we greet each other ceremoniously while ignoring the presence of one who is obviously poor. This covers our guilty feelings of being part of those who "have" when perhaps we don't feel deserving. Ignoring the poor will not take care of our guilt. There are always contradictory guilt feelings going on in us, especially in this area.

Judgment is ever present, whether we're rich or poor. The problem is not as much in poverty and wealth as in the inevitable comparisons that people mutually make. Jesus had a lot to say about judging others, and we need to remind ourselves of this constantly (Matt. 7:1-5).

The family finances provide the fuel for the major disagreements in a marriage. In one statewide survey of Christians, financial matters were cited as the major cause of conflict. Some examples are as follows:

a. Money is often used by one or both partners as an emotional club to control or punish the other. When a person, male or female, feels threatened, his natural instinct is to somehow survive. Many times if a woman feels that she is being shortchanged in her position, she will turn to the most powerful weapon she controls—she withholds sex.

b. The husband is likely to hold back money to prove his domination or in retaliation of her withholding sex. Traditionally, men have been responsible for handling the family finances because women were not supposed to understand money. Some men withhold money or even the household allowance to "punish" what they consider misbehavior, thus treating their wife as a child rather than an adult.

c. A working wife may exercise control over her husband by

keeping what she earns as "hers" and what he makes as "ours." Her financial independence makes it possible for her to leave.

d.  An inordinate desire or demand for money may indicate an emotional need that is not being met. Many times we turn to money as a love substitute. Money and the things money buys become symbols of our ego. When the money is low, our ego and self-worth are shattered.

e.  Money can be used as a tool in manipulating all members of the family. If one controls the finances, he can control the family. Equal responsibility for financial matters should be the rule for a secure family.

Financial planning is an absolute necessity. Bill Ginn, assistant manager, advanced financial planning, and a deacon at Wieuca Road Baptist Church, offers the following suggestions. First, pray about this undertaking. Second, identify your objectives, both short- and long-range, and translate them into a plan. Third, gather all the information you can that is pertinent to the objectives (financial statements, tax forms, and legal documents). Fourth, analyze your present position and consider viable alternatives. Fifth, develop and implement your plan based upon a thorough appraisal of the above. Sixth, review and revise your plan on a regular basis—ideally, once a year or after any major change in financial status.

The Bible tells us how we are to spend our money. We are to provide for the needs of our family (1 Tim. 5:8). We are also to pay our debts promptly (2 Kings 4:7). We can use our money to help others (1 John 3:17; Acts 2:45; 4:34). As Christians, we are God's stewards and are entrusted with his money (1 Cor. 4:2). The proper handling of our finances is a key to spiritual fruit in our lives (Luke 16:10).

Remember that figures don't lie. You either have money or you don't. Be realistic in facing up to facts. Face this part of your life together, both being equally involved with no hidden agendas. "His" and "hers" look good on towels, but cannot be applied to money. Try to understand the other's emotional reactions to money.

The partner who is best qualified to handle the family finances should assume the responsibility. It may be that the one who has the best training for the job simply does not have the time to do all that is necessary (going to the bank, writing checks, etc.). Rather than use several evenings or a day off to do this "work," the spouse who has the less demanding schedule can learn to do this and both can enjoy the free time together. Sometimes finances become an emotional problem for the bookkeeper of the family. So it becomes a matter of who is best suited in ability, temperament, and time. It is not a sex-oriented task.

*Priorities* need to be agreed upon and then reevaluated periodically. If a new house is top on the priority list of both spouses, then both will be willing to sacrifice in some area to save for that common goal. Don't put aside all pleasures now while young or in midlife, saving for the golden retirement years. Save prudently, but remember that we must enjoy doing things, going places, being with each other now; we may forget how to have fun if we don't stay in practice.

Communication quickly becomes strangled when one spends selfishly (golf clubs, a fur coat, gambling, fishing trip for one, etc.) and both are on the defensive. Family backgrounds that differ greatly in the way finances were used impede communication between the couple. Perhaps she never had to do anything but ask Daddy for money and he gave it to her. Now she can't understand why she can't have everything she wants *now*. He may be from a depression-scarred family where every nickel is examined and each expense weighed carefully. There need to be lengthy, open, unemotional conversations, during which time each tells the other about these family characteristics so each will know where the other is coming from. Understand that there is a tremendous carryover from the way money was handled in the parental family.

Be sure to make a will. Do this right away. It can ease the problems that sudden death could bring.

Money problems for re-wed couples seem to be endless. It would be very rare for anyone to be involved to the point of marriage with a person who has been previously married without facing financial reality. Only a very wealthy person can really afford to maintain two homes.

When a widow thinks of remarriage, she very often has to decide whether the relationship is worth the price of losing some financial benefits that will cease when she remarries. If she is young and has young children, this may put a severe psychological strain on the relationship. Her new husband may feel under great pressure to make her happy and the children satisfied. Hopefully, the period of courtship was long enough to work through these feelings and for her to marry him with no intention of holding "look what I gave up" over his head.

A divorced woman in a new marriage situation may soon realize that one thing is still the same—money. Only now it's even more complicated. In a few instances alimony is still granted to a woman in divorce, but usually it is in the form of child support. Of course, the alimony will stop once she remarries, but the child support will continue. The father of the children is responsible for his share of their support. We all know cases where getting child support from a former spouse is like pulling teeth. He (sometimes she) receives some sort of pleasure from forcing the former spouse to beg or resort to court action. Sometimes he will leave the state to avoid paying. Any of these situations will put an emotional and financial burden on the new family.

It is quite possible that the new spouse is a divorced father who has to pay child support. If his new wife's children live with them and they have trouble getting the child support for her children, he will end up having to care for both families. What a drain! What anger will be boiling! Unless he is wealthy, there will be a great financial crunch; and if his new wife is not already working, she will surely have to do so. Even very gracious and loving women who have faced this realistically still have twinges of resentment. All of us are human, and this very obvious reminder (automatically subtracting a substantial amount) comes at least once a month. Unless both husband and wife can be totally open to each other about their feelings, this can be big trouble or at least food for a monthly depression. It is one thing to realistically assume this responsibility; but there will be times when it is difficult not to be resentful (if you're feeling too tired to work; hate your job; the relationship is not rewarding, etc.). This makes the spouse (usually the husband) feel frustrated and responsible for the unhappiness.

Another situation that can aggravate the money situation (when the budget is tight) occurs when the children who are in the custody of the ex-spouse come to visit. The need to "entertain" them can mean large or small expenditures of money budgeted for necessities. Sometimes on a rainy day, the only way to escape a small apartment and survive is to go to a movie or find some other entertainment. Of course, there are museums and such, but the average child is not that happy about so much culture!

If both husband and wife are salaried with few investments, it is very realistic to assume that it will be many years before it will be feasible to own a home. Usually the man, as a result of the property settlement, lost the house to his previous wife and so lost any accumulated equity for further housing investment. It is hard not to be able to dream with some early time schedule about owning a home.

Even more difficult to manage emotionally is being caught in the trap of having to pay off outstanding debts of a previous marriage. This can be devastating, financially and emotionally. One has to continually work on being forgiving in order not to become bitter.

Each family has to settle these situations in the best way for all concerned. However, remember that it is important to face the facts and make plans accordingly. Keep the lines of communication open, and be helpful and understanding to each other.

Most of all, I urge the use of a trusted family counselor as an uninvolved person who can hear your pain and resentment and allow you to be human in your feelings. Don't punish yourself for not having all your hard feelings and anger taken care of once and for all. You have permission to feel, but take care of it constructively. You cannot *not* afford counseling to keep yourself and your marriage together. Ask your pastor or someone on your church staff to help you find the kind of help you need.

Another threat and barrier to communication in marriage is unresolved hostility toward parents and unresolved dependence on parents. Marriage requires a couple to make an emotional transfer from parents to spouse. In some cases this is quite simple, but in others it is painful and requires years to accomplish. A young couple, unused to responsibilities, may become resentful; and one partner or the other, or both, may run home to Mother or threaten to do so. The marital family must take precedence over the biological family.

Parents have ways of both subtly and overtly encouraging their married children to cling to them. Some parents have trouble cutting the umbilical cord and fail to realize that they are not successful parents until their children are on their own, functioning as mature adults. Can you recognize the potential dangers in these situations?

a.  A wife is used to being protected by her parents and when problems, large or small, arise in her marriage relationship, she runs to her mother for advice. Sometimes this is fostered by the mother.

b.  A husband feels that his mother "needs" him (his mother makes sure that he senses this) and gives more time and attention to his mother than to his wife.

c.  A mother may buy clothes for her married daughter on a consistent basis without consulting her about her preferences. She infers (whether intentional or not) that the husband is not able to provide for her daughter. (This is apart from Christmas or other gift times.)

d.  A mother may voice her concern that her son is living in a dirty house, wearing unironed shirts, not having proper food, etc., and in some way hint that he would be better off back home with his parents.

e.   The real test comes when grandchildren appear and each side of the family has definite ideas about child rearing. Very likely neither side will suit the couple. Hopefully, they can stand united against the onslaught.

f.   In-law and parent problems are complicated by financial aid given to the young couple. The aid should be given with no strings attached, even though this is difficult.

g.   Husband and wife need to establish their own identity. This cannot be done if the in-laws claim every dinner or drop by at all times of the day and night or expect more than normal visiting.

It is important for a married couple to handle relationships with parents and in-laws on a positive basis. We need to (1) remember that family ties are normal and important and that it is helpful to make the process of separating themselves gradual rather than abrupt; (2) understand the spouse's concern for his parents; (3) accept in a mature way the fact that parents cannot automatically stop caring about their children just because the latter get married and that parental help can sometimes be a wonderful thing to have; (4) present a united front to any attempt by parents or in-laws to interfere, remembering that firmness is more effective than hostility.

As a marriage grows, the mutual love and support the relationship gives to husband and wife gradually replace a person's dependence on his parents. Each new responsibility carried out, each goal achieved, strengthens the ego. In this way the rewards of marriage take precedence over childhood satisfactions. And a really fortunate couple will make the transition with their parents' help.

## Work Space

The first two questions are to be discussed by the large group. First, divide into small groups (four people, not couples) and be prepared to report back to the whole group.

1.  Discuss the different ways of interpreting this greeting. Set the stage: She has been waiting for him to come home, trying to keep dinner hot. He is later than usual, caught in traffic, tired and weary.

    "Where have you *been*?" "*Where* have you been?" "Where *have* you been?"

    Does he hear concern? Does he hear accusation? Does she want apology? Will he react with attack? Is she smiling or frowning? Does she reach out to him or turn her back? Does she want a lingering embrace?

2.  Discuss some of the common courtesies that are forgotten after the honeymoon. Add to the ones mentioned in the material and be ready to brainstorm this problem with the larger group. Do you think that this lack of good manners toward each other can be indicative of deeper problems? If so, how?

3.  Marriage counselors indicate that among newlywed couples there need to be ways of understanding the background of each other. For instance, to one "beans" may mean "green beans"; to the other "beans" means "dried navy beans cooked with ham." To one, Christmas may mean extravagant splurging on gifts for everyone and big family gatherings. For the other it may mean a very depressing time, being lonely.

    Suggest ways to get information and understanding.
    Do the next question individually.

4. Remember how your family handled money:
   a. When you were growing up, did you receive an allowance? _____

      If so, at what age did you begin to receive it? _____ Did you receive an allowance as payment for certain chores? _____ Or did you receive it just for existing? _____

   b. Were you punished by having your allowance taken away? _____

   c. Were you taught how to handle money responsibly? _____

   d. Did you learn about tithing by seeing your parents give to the church? _____

   e. Through your college years, did your parents always bail you out of any money trouble? _____

   f. Do you remember seeing your father at the dining table or desk writing checks and knowing that you should stay clear? _____

   g. Did your mother always have to beg for money for extras? _____

   h. Did you have a job during high school and college? _____

   i. Did you save money for a purpose? _____

   Now turn your chairs so that each couple can talk easily without being disturbed by the group and talk about the next question. (If time is short, this should be done at home.)

5. Talk about the ways your parental families handled money. Take turns telling each other facts about this. Make no judgments on either family; just tell each other about it. Remember some significant occasions when finances were a critical issue.

   Again, divide into small groups of four people each (no couples) to discuss the next question.

6. Discuss some problems that could come about because of in-laws. Do these affect the communication level of a couple? How can this be handled?

   If time allows, have each couple again move chairs so that they can talk without being disturbed.

7. Tell each other two things that create problems with you concerning your in-laws. Why do you think that it is difficult to maintain open communication when in-laws are present? Can you help each other with this?

   At home:
8. Go over these questions together.
   1. Each one write down one nonessential you'd like to splurge on. Is this reasonable or out of the question?
   2. What are your needs, wants, and wishes?
   3. Do you have a workable budget? Do you have any/many charge accounts? Do you limit your expenditures by your income?
   4. Do you make a practice of spending large sums of money without consulting each other? Lie about what an item cost?
   5. Are you planning an insurance program or a specific investment plan?
   6. Marriage should mean the consolidation of finances, plans, dreams, friends, and especially a sense of values. Is this true of yours?

7. Can you talk reasonably and calmly about money matters, or do you use money as a club to prove a point?

8. Accepting financial aid from one or both parents may be a problem. How can you deal with this?

9. Have you made plans in your budget for Christmas and birthday gifts?

10. Have you been able to come to an understanding about checking accounts and savings?

11. Do you have separate checking accounts? Savings accounts? Is this reasonable? Do you want your spouse to have either a savings or checking account that is separate? Does this threaten you? Can you discuss this openly? Try to do so this week.

12. Those who are re-wed need to take a long hard look at finances.

    a. Discuss the pain of money problems. Understand that underlying much of the emotional strain of this new family relationship will be financial commitments to a former family or the embarrassment of not receiving child support on time (or at all).

    b. If you have not changed your will (or have never made one) do not wait another day. You owe this to all for whom you have some responsibility, particularly your children and your new spouse. Both husband and wife need to do this.

# 5.  Nurturing Intimacy

*Bible Passages:*          Matthew 19:4-6; Ephesians 5:28-33;
                           1 Corinthians 13:4-13

> "Set me as a seal upon your heart
> . . . for love is strong as death . . .
> Many waters cannot quench love,
> neither can floods drown it."
>                                   (Song of Solomon 8:6-7, RSV)

*I*ntimacy is the interlocking of two individuals by a bond that is so fragile and intangible that it is frightening. Intimacy in the deepest, most rewarding relationship is not only a *horizontal* relationship, but also must have a *vertical* dimension. The spiritual depth of each person nurtures the relationship. Moments of sharing on a spiritual level are truly precious and allow the partner to see to the depths of the soul of the loved one. This is not the type of "sharing" you do in a group discussion or in just telling someone about your troubles and receiving assurance. This is an opening of the door to your soul and allowing your spouse to see inside. At some point he will do the same. This is the ultimate type of intimacy that comes only after a depth of trust and understanding has been developed and tested.

A relationship where there is growing intimacy doesn't just happen—it is the result of the self-investment of two people who are determined to work at the relationship and turn problems into possibilities. The art of relating in-depth cannot be left unattended or left to grow without food and water. It will fade and die, either quickly or by a slow, torturous death.

Developing intimacy is costly, but the rewards are unbelievably rich. The sweetest satisfaction available to human beings comes through the process of working together to strengthen and deepen the marriage relationship.

Intimacy does not necessarily grow in a continuous upward spiral. There are times of drought when the soil of the relationship seems barren and hard. Hang in there and keep working; learn irrigation methods; and the lush seasons will come again and be even more beautiful and satisfying.

When one spouse complains, "I'm not being fulfilled," it may be a legitimate cry for help and time for help from a professional counselor. On the other hand, it may be time for patience and learning how to deal creatively with a specific period of time in the relationship. Remember that nothing ever stays the same. We can do a lot to help this be a time of growth.

Intimacy in marriage can bring ecstasy, mutual satisfaction, well-being, joy, serenity, and peace. Intimacy is closeness and unity, presupposing warmth and love. Intimacy is grace; it is refusing to turn away or hide from each other. Intimacy is also forgiveness. Forgiveness is the means of rebuilding a relationship which has been broken or strained. Intimacy is different for different people. One couple may find satisfaction and intimacy in a comfortable, companionable marriage. Another may find that it is a tumultuous relationship, balanced with intense passion and vigorous battles. Intimacy provides meaning in lonely lives. "To love and to cherish" commits the couple to agree to become the key resource person to each other. It is a commitment to the mutual responsibility for fulfilling the deep personality needs of the other. We must fill this function by developing a relationship deep enough to provide channels for satisfying personality hungers.

Nurturing one's partner can be an exciting experience in participating in the creative process of giving, as well as receiving, love. It is in the process of interaction, the giving/receiving, that one's basic needs are satisfied.

**We need to feel worthy and accepted.** Accepting each other's vulnerable and touchy areas means that we are aware of those areas and respect the other enough not to trample over them. Acceptance is the ability to love your spouse just as he is without assuming that you can change him or that living with you will work miracles. One young wife put it this way: "I need to know that he loves me for what I am deep down inside . . . that he really likes me, likes being with me."

**We need to feel secure, to feel a sense of belonging and being wanted.** This feeling of security is acknowledged in the marriage vows—"for better or for worse." This means that in moments of anger or desperation, neither succumbs to the use of threats to leave in order to manipulate the other. The need for stability and continuity in marriage must be met because all around things are in a state of flux. Husband and wife, in order to have any kind of relationship, must know that they will stand by each other (not parents or children or friends) through all circumstances, good and bad, happy and sorrowful, in conflicts, through sickness, loss of job, through the crises some teenage children can bring, and on and on.

**We need to be needed and to love.** Marriage is the place to invest your life in someone else. Be ever attuned to the needs of your spouse. When your mate has been hurt or bruised by disappointment or grief and needs affection, your response should be a spontaneous reaching out to give love and assurance. Husband and wife need to be aware of the other's needs and frustrations. This is not one-sided. Sometime try honestly to put yourself in the other's shoes and try to understand something of what your spouse experiences.

**We need to have self-esteem strengthened.** Each spouse needs to know that he is valued by the other. Harsh words, "put-downs," and forgetting a birthday or anniversary are some of the ways of bruising the ego of your mate. Negative cycles start this way. When hurts begin to add up, the ego is shattered. A friend recently said, "My husband makes me feel good about myself." Now that man has a great thing going. She, in turn, will do her best to do the same for him! I guess a good way to put it is being appreciated by each other. What you do to strengthen your partner's self-esteem will increase his ability to give in the relationship.

One form of strengthening the self-esteem of your spouse is to affirm his sense of sexual attractiveness. No hurt is deeper than a slur or attack on one's sexual adequacy. Develop the art of giving verbal and silent compliments—for example, a husband bringing his wife a gift of her (their) favorite cologne or bath powder. He is saying powerfully, "I'm glad you're a woman and I'm a man and I enjoy the fact that you are very much a woman!"

**We need freedom to grow.** Partners need to allow each other the inner freedom to grow toward the potential God gave them. This has to be within the rhythm of marriage—never letting one's freedom become a stumbling block to the other or to the relationship. There is a fine line, and each couple must learn where the bounds are.

**We need pleasures of the mind and body**—sexual, intellectual, aesthetic, interpersonal, and spiritual.

**Sexual play and ecstasy and satisfaction** can infuse the total marriage relationship with zest and beauty and greater appreciation of each other. The ecstatic pleasure of sex and also the relaxation (letting one's hair down) gives a mini-vacation from the burdens of adult responsibility. It is the ultimate experience of sharing and self-abandon, of trusting, in the merging of husband and wife. The biblical phrase is "to become one flesh."

**Intellectual intimacy** is the closeness related to the world of ideas—sharing a study, reading a book and discussing it, attending a lecture, or allowing each other to have views and express them without negating the validity of the other's ideas. This is where one spouse can outgrow the other intellectually. You've heard of one spouse putting the other through college or graduate school, only to have the relationship disintegrate. This doesn't have to happen if there is a mutual respect for each other's intellectual capacities and both make an effort to grow intellectually together.

**Aesthetic intimacy** is the sharing of beauty—a marvelous view; listening to a symphony; the tranquility of the sunset; whatever the experience may be—a communion for the couple.

**Work intimacy** entails the common tasks of running a home, earning a living, and community and church responsibilities. Work intimacy needs to be balanced with other forms of intimacy, especially recreational intimacy (sports, movies, games, whatever both partners enjoy doing). Achieving short-term and long-term goals provides great satisfaction and adds to the total intimacy of the relationship. Many couples get caught on this work intimacy and fail to develop any other area of their lives.

**Creative intimacy** is not only conceiving and parenting children, but really the experience of helping each other grow. That doesn't mean to "reform" each other.

**Spiritual intimacy** is more than continuing religious tradition. It is acknowledging individual relationship to God. Through this spiritual relationship, appreciation for each other is deepened and strengthened. It also gives both a sense of direction, a firm foundation.

Marriage is not meant to provide a hiding place for two people, even though this may seem peaceful at times. A person living alone becomes set in his ways and often merely marks time. Marriage, at its best, is a demanding confrontation in which both husband and wife must constantly be developing and growing in their understanding of each other and of themselves.

Each spouse has great power to starve or nourish the other. No one can make the other person happy, but we do promise to provide the interpersonal food necessary to feed the needs of each other.

Each spouse must be an independent, coping individual. The independent person likes himself and others and enjoys contact with other people. It takes a person with self-respect to respect another. It takes one who can walk alone to be able to walk in step with another.

Learn to react to the here and now. This is essential for intimacy. Be ready to drop other concerns and thoughts and listen. Learn to appreciate the beauties of nature; develop your senses—touch, smell, etc.

A couple who desires a deep relationship must be willing to give more of themselves to keep the openness, equality, communication, and companionship alive. Learn to be emotionally present to each other. We can identify with the wife who complains, "I feel like you are still at the office—or somewhere" or the husband who says, "Why should I tell you anything? You don't really listen to me." Cultivate the quality of presence.

Trust and commitment to each other (fidelity and continuity), "for better or worse," are absolutely essential to any development of intimacy. The "for better or worse" demands that we use periods of crisis, estrangement, conflict, or any difficult time to work even harder at deepening the relationship.

Learn to care deeply for each other. Find ways to express your caring. Your spouse must know that he is the most important person in your life. Show that you care—give your best to each other.

Deep sharing is overwhelming and rare. So many fears stand in the way. What if my spouse does not sense the tremendous importance of this moment? It is too painful to risk being mocked or not heard. The emotional solitude of the one who tried to share and was rebuffed is terrible.

The kind of love that is described in the thirteenth chapter of 1 Corinthians is filled with wonder, tenderness, passion, comfort, and confrontation, and is always growing. Intimacy in marriage assumes the kind of love that is a maturing, always adventurous sharing, becoming richer and more satisfying with the passing of time. The intimate love so desired in marriage requires time and a continuing courtship. Intimacy is not a goal to be met but a road to travel together.

Include in your prayer time together a prayer like this:

Heavenly Father, _____and I thank you for
bringing us together. Thank you for giving us the Christlike
qualities of loving and caring for each other. Help us to grow
throughout our lives in our capacity to love and understand
each other. Keep us close to thee. In Jesus' name. Amen.

## Work Space

Ask yourself these questions:
1. Does this relationship leave me with feelings of increased strength and value or of weakness and self-rejection?
2. How do you feel about your marriage? Do you have feelings of warmth and acceptance or coldness and unhappiness? Why do you think you feel the way you do?

As a couple:

Tell each other what you like and admire about the other. How can you make the most of these strengths in increasing the intimacy between you?

When you experience conflict in your marriage, try to interrupt the negative cycle. Remember that needs of one or both are not being met.
a. Try to ascertain in your own mind and together what is missing at this point (affection, sexual satisfaction, affirmation, etc.).
b. Decide which needs are exclusively one-sided and which overlap. Now begin to work on those areas which overlap, and the negative cycle will be broken.
c. Decide positive ways to achieve the goals of meeting mutual needs. This will lead to lessening differences in other areas.

Two groups discuss the following questions and report:
1. How can a couple overcome the walls in their marriage, replacing them with bridges?



2. How can a couple stimulate the growth of creative closeness and increase their skills in intimate relating?

3.  Decide on a problem a couple may encounter such as:
    husband discovers wife has been married before, which
    he didn't know before marriage; wife resents mother-in-
    law buying (selecting) furniture and presenting it to them;
    husband and wife have difficulty agreeing on discipline of
    children (from previous marriage). Now reverse role
    play—husband play wife's role and vice versa as a way to
    better understanding.

# 6. *Talk, Touch, Listen*

*Bible Passages:* 1 Corinthians 13; Matthew 5:22; Psalm 19:14

One of the characters in Lillian Hellman's play *Toys in the Attic* says, "People change and forget to tell each other." Talking, touching, and listening are all very vital in the communication system in the home, office, school, or wherever you have any contact with people. Perhaps another element should be added—look or watch. Remember these four words constantly—talk, touch, listen, and look. As long as we're alive we're in the communicating business. As we have said, you cannot *not* communicate. Communication will either be positive or negative. We really want to heighten the sensitivity of individuals so that each one will be aware of the needs and signals of the other. What a satisfying, warm feeling to know that my spouse is going to be aware of my feelings and will understand me! Remember that you can only talk to a person when he is open to communication—only on a subject he is willing to communicate about—and only in a manner he considers appropriate.

Talking is the chief way we have of revealing ourselves to others. This is also the chief way we have of trying to control or change another. Words are used to cover up feelings of warmth and tenderness. So often a couple (even a whole family) will develop a pattern of verbal abuse, each one trying to top the other with sarcasm and accusation. They forget how much they really care about each other and become fearful of exposing their true feelings. They are afraid of ridicule in case the other continues to respond with verbal abuse.

Hostility is openly communicated with words. The purpose is to hurt each other, and words are indelibly written in the mind and on the heart when hurled in heated anger. Words like these: (a) "You never do anything right; you're a mess; you're getting more like your mother every day." (b) "You do that one more time and see what happens!" This veiled threat is devastating to a relationship. (c) "How can you be so stupid?"

Uncomplimentary labels are threatening to one's ego and self-esteem. Labeling a husband or wife as neurotic, narrow-minded, prudish, etc., really limits our understanding of that person. Labeling is used by talkers to avoid thinking. Remember the Scripture Matthew 5:22, "And whosoever shall say to his brother, Raca, shall be in danger of the council, but whosoever shall say, Thou fool, shall be in danger of hell fire" (KJV).

Words such as "I want your advice" or "What do you think?" or "I'd like to discuss this with you" illustrate one's ability to seek the opinion of others. They declare that you are open to hearing the viewpoint of others. It is oppressing to have a spouse who knows everything already.

"Aren't you ashamed of yourself?" is a phrase most often used by parents to children, but in some subtle ways husbands and wives use shame to control each other and to drive true feelings underground. "I have done so much for you" intimates that you will surely do what I want out of pity. Pity is not the tool to use to enforce demands. Fear is a great motivator for children and adults. Threats of "What will people think?" are probably more fearful than the wrath of God. These are effective fear- and guilt-inducing means of communication.

Talk to each other. Find times during each day to talk to each other, at least fifteen minutes, to find out what's going on inside you. At some point, perhaps at dinner, make a habit of each one telling about *your happiest time during the day*. This is a good positive way to establish communicative conversation. It is a very good habit to establish early and to continue when there are children. It can be a creative, happy time which can also be used as a family worship time. It is healthy to keep as much communication as possible on a positive note to counterbalance the negative that naturally occurs.

The most difficult communication is sex talk. It is possible to experience sexual intercourse and enjoy it, but many cannot discuss the situation without accusations or hurtful words. It is important to learn early to be open and uninhibited, not only in actions but also in verbal communication concerning this part of life. A man or woman is never more alone than when he or she is locked in a loveless sexual embrace. Without their talking things out, this experience can become nothing more than a frustrating, unfulfilling game, rather than a unifying, satisfying, precious experience.

The intimacy of lovemaking prompts a couple to talk. It provides quiet hours of conversation and fuses the emotions of the couple together. It introduces them to a wholly different and infinite dimension of intimacy.

Marriage counselors hear these emotion-charged words frequently: "He hasn't touched me in months." "She only allows me to hold her when she wants me to buy her something." "He only touches me when he wants sex. He doesn't care about me as a person."

Touching is a basic human need. Babies thrive on the holding, loving care of parents. Studies have shown over and over again that babies who are held while nursed or bottle-fed grow and respond well, while those who are *only* fed by a propped bottle become listless and are not well emotionally or physically. Some hospitals have hired people to be substitute parents or grandparents to come in and feed and hold babies who have no one to care for them. We never outgrow the need for being touched lovingly. The more emotional deprivation a person experiences in childhood, the harder it will be for him to give love as an adult. The more love, trust, and security a person receives as a child, the more he will be able to give love as an adult.

Some families are very reserved, expressing very little emotional warmth to each other. For a person who has grown up in this atmosphere, it may be difficult to express warmth to anyone, even a spouse. Some people who have grown up in a very "puritan" home where no one touched, either to punish or to love, find it difficult to suddenly change and realize it is all right and necessary to touch and love one's spouse. It's the idea of "nice people don't," and help is needed in overcoming this attitude.

Have you ever seen a "cowed" dog who is afraid to approach any human being? It is a sad sight. You can almost read what is going on inside: *A pat on the head would feel nice, but the last time a human got near, he kicked me. . . . What to do?* Every year there are children who are maimed and bruised by abusive parents. This cripples emotionally as well as physically. It is sad but true that there are people who have experienced mistreatment and are emotionally crippled from the experience. They need competent help to work this out. A spouse cannot assume responsibility for the type of therapy needed.

There are also couples who mistreat each other physically. It may sound farfetched and like something you only read about in the newspaper, but it is not uncommon for a husband or wife to abuse the other physically. Every counselor, pastor, and psychiatrist hears and sees the evidence of physical abuse more frequently than can be imagined. Sometimes this shows up early in the marriage and sometimes occurs later, possibly as a result of years of frustration. A counselor-friend told me recently of a young couple, married less than a year, who sought his help because the husband beat the wife. There is great hope for them because they came for help early and together and he is afraid of his inappropriate behavior.

Many times it is the wife who sends her husband to work with scratches, cuts, and bruises on his face. Fingernails are marvelous weapons. This is not at all unusual. Jealousy is often the trigger for this type of reaction. One man couldn't deal with his wife's incessant badgering and nagging and nearly choked her to death when he had all he could take.

She never figured out why he did this, and he was so ashamed that they finally divorced.

Very often couples can be helped in dealing with each other and their frustrations. At the first sign of inappropriate behavior, seek competent help. You (as a couple) can be trained to rationally learn what triggers this violent behavior, reprogram yourselves, and learn an appropriate response to each other. Other behavior that falls into this category is breaking furniture, throwing dishes (anything), or any type of physically violent actions. Those are very frightening to all involved in this experience; the one doing the violence, the victim, and anyone else in the household.

Any type of acted-out violence such as has been mentioned is a mere symptom of deep psychological problems. This is not a condemnation but an acknowledgment that "nice" people can have these problems. The only condemnation comes when they do not acknowledge this problem and seek help. Also, the victim quickly becomes crippled emotionally (and possibly physically) if he allows this action to continue without seeking help.

Now let's look at the beautiful side of touching. The art of touching can be learned as an adult if it didn't come with your family background. A hug, squeeze, or pat appropriately placed can do wonders to lift the spirit. If you're slaving over a hot stove, a gentle nuzzle will make it all worthwhile.

Many women have complained that any touching leads immediately to jumping in bed. This shouldn't be necessarily so. All our actions and responses fuse together to create the desire for sexual intimacy, but there are lots of times when the sexual act itself may be hours away. Loving looks, words, and touches should be enjoyed whenever appropriate without demanding or expecting instant sex. The coming together in sexual intercourse is like the dessert at dinner time; the other courses come first. If you eat the dessert first, it is enjoyable, but you'll be hungry again in a few minutes. The basic meat and potatoes make the dessert more satisfying. All the delightful hugs, kisses, pats, snuggles, and nuzzles experienced make life worth living. Without these expressions of affection, you might as well be single and living with a roommate.

Bedtime is important in the making or breaking of a marriage. It is true that some people have very definite sleep habits and rituals that they observe on getting ready for and going to bed. When you marry, some of those patterns may have to be altered in order to achieve the desired results in bed and in marriage as a whole. Yes, you can change old habits. It is important to be desirable. No one wants to get in the same bed with a dirty, sweaty, prickly person or a head full of curlers or a greasy face. Make yourself touchable. It is one of the joys of marriage to snuggle, to touch in some way before going to sleep. You may turn your back on your spouse, but not before you've expressed affection or acknowledged his presence somehow. Going to bed together and never touching is a very lonely experience. Be sensitive to the expectations, needs, and desires of each other. Don't be stingy with expressions of love. Being generous with your touches and kind words will bring huge dividends. It will be worth any changes you have to make in your old habits. Begin to think of what your spouse would like—how to please and delight him—and you'll plant seeds that will bloom and become more lovely as the years go by. Selfishness will bring its own reward—isolation and loneliness.

What appears to be a sexual adventure is often the result of broken communication between husband and wife. We forget how to talk and how to listen and how to be sensitive to each other. Many a woman who discovers that her husband is having an affair assumes the woman is a young, beautiful, sexy blonde. That is true in many cases; however, just as often the woman may be older, a little dowdy, and dumpy! What is her charm? She gives him her full attention, hanging on his every word. Husbands and wives need to give undivided attention to each other.

Chronic busyness is a way that people can legitimately

avoid having to sit down and really listen to each other. Many times this is one-sided. The wife can be slam-banging in the kitchen or running the vacuum, or the husband can find something that has to be worked on in the garage or base-ment. Both are doing good things while avoiding each other. Each one is finding a way to keep from relating in-depth.

There are a lot of reasons for not listening to each other. (1) Some people are notoriously bad listeners. They hear only what they want to hear. They may pick up a word or two out of a paragraph and understand an entirely different meaning than was intended. (2) We tune people out sometimes because we're lazy and don't want to be bothered, and some-times because the person talking maintains a constant chatter and conceals any important point with so much wrapping that we throw it all out as packing. (3) We get focused on our own inner problems and forget that the world is going on around us. Other people (even a spouse) cannot break into this ring of isolation. (4) We get absorbed in something else; a problem at work, a child, etc. Everyone around us is supposed to know what we're thinking about and leave us undisturbed. (5) Sometimes we don't listen because we're afraid of what we may hear. If we don't "hear" it, perhaps it will pass.

We can learn to listen and also to communicate so that we'll be heard. Learn alternative phrases such as: "It seems to me"; "I may be wrong, but I think . . ." rather than "You know in your heart" or "Everybody with any sense knows."

"I feel that your part of the housework is not being done and this hurts me" rather than "You lazy slob, why don't you get off the sofa and help with the work around here?"

"I wish you would stay home and be with me tonight" rather than "You never stay home; you always go out with your friends and I have to stay here alone."

Lofton Hudson says, "You cannot communicate with a person . . . unless he is open at that time to the receiving of signals. Broadcasting when there is no receiver is futile."[1] Remember that timing is all-important. Never try to discuss a

## Work Space

Divide into groups of four—not couples. Discuss the first two questions.

1. One area of communication problems that occurs with discouraging frequency is that each spouse carried patterns of noncommunication from parents over into his own marriage. He assumes that "everyone" does it this way. Example: Barbara has many problems and differences with her husband but cannot get him to talk about them. "He won't ever argue with me about anything; he won't even discuss things." Bob's father and mother were neutral to each other—indifferent. He never took his troubles to them as a child. He grew up holding everything in. Can this situation be helped? Make suggestions.

2. Discuss things that can be a block to communication and think of ways to increase the opportunities for communication. For example: lack of time together—when running errands, go together. Report to larger group.

Together—as a couple:
3. Make specific plans for improving your communication this week in the area discussed (talk, touch, listen). Write down at least one way to accomplish this during the week.

4. To think about and discuss this week: Can you predict
   how your spouse would react in a crisis? For example:
   You have an automobile accident, no injuries, but plenty
   of damage to both cars. Or you go to the doctor and
   discover that you will have to have major surgery (not
   cancer). Or you discover you're pregnant and this was not
   planned for this time in your life. Can you trust your
   spouse?

5. Write down two nonverbal communications you receive
   from your spouse: one giving a happy, positive message,
   the other giving a negative message. Share these with
   each other.

# 7. How to Fuss and/or Fight Fairly
## (Grace and Forgiveness— The Miracle)

*Bible Passages:*   Ephesians 4:26; Luke 15:28-32; Genesis 37:4; John 1:14-18; Psalm 32:1-5; 103; Hebrews 4:15; Ephesians 4:32; Matthew 18; 5:23-24; 6:14-15; Luke 16:15; 23:24

## How to Fuss and/or Fight Fairly

*I*f there is an ideal marriage, it is not because the two persons involved are ideal but because they have worked and continually work to creatively deal with differences. They have learned to accept the frailty of human nature *and* the goodness of God. They have learned to smile at themselves and, thus, at each other with love.

Remember that all families have double lives—the public view, which is shown to neighbors, co-workers, and the world; and the private, complicated relationships in the home. Each member of the family experiences a desperate struggle for individual survival. We are forever at different stages in our reaching out, drawing back, "becoming," and it is unlikely that we will ever be at the same point as our spouse.

When a marriage has disintegrated, it didn't happen because of one devastating event but because that event brought the sad state of the marriage to the inescapable attention of the couple. Approximately one-half of the divorces in America occur in marriages of less than six years. Physical attraction alone is not enough to build a marriage on. Building a marriage is somewhat comparable to building a house. When it is completed, you don't see all the materials that went into the construction—the foundation blocks, steel, concrete, insulation, 4 x 4's, wiring, subflooring, staples, nails, primer paint, pipes, and all the other vital materials that make it workable, livable, and pleasant. Some couples simply do not have the proper materials for a workable marriage. Others do not give themselves enough time to work through all the adjustments and integration of two people coming together.

This becomes even more critical when this is a second marriage. All the material must be extra strong to begin with; and then it will take an unusual amount of energy to build the marriage. A second marriage deserves a longer "completion date" also. (I realize there is never a completion date for a marriage, but am speaking in terms of building a house.) There will probably be a lot more "painting and fixing up" of this marriage because of previous experience, as well as trying to integrate two families, which may include children.

Every marriage has its bad days, its boring times, the crisis times. This is part of the interweaving pattern of life. The good days, happy times generally overlay the troubled times; and they all become part of the fabric of life.

It is natural and logical that there will be times when a husband and wife differ enough to argue. As a general rule it would be safe to say that couples who insist that they do not have any differences have one spouse who is overwhelmingly dominant and the other docile enough to go along; or they could both be very "blah" and unopinionated; or they may have worked out a satisfactory arrangement in dealing with differences. We'll talk more about this as we go along.

How can a Christian couple handle family fusses? Too often we are told that if we are true-blue Christians we will not get mad, not get upset; we are to control ourselves and think positively. It sounds fine, but if we're honest it means that we become hypocritical and resentful. We store up our feelings and eventually explode one way or another; we develop ulcers, a rash, or other physical problems; or there is the possibility of violence.

Anger is a normal part of life. It is nothing to be ashamed of (perhaps only the way we deal with it). Anger and hostility are the causes or the results of poor communication. If the partners are afraid to face the anger and work it through, serious trouble begins to seep into the relationship. You have probably noticed some signs of this in other couples: "cutting each other down," even in the presence of others; a raging "cold" war; psychosomatic illnesses which stem from misplaced anger (turning anger inward and thus manipulating the other). Sexual problems can often be traced to unresolved anger. Adults often have temper tantrums which result in various forms of aggression as the result of the inability to express rage appropriately.

Anger, when kept under cover, will finally explode. This may occur in the ways already mentioned, or it may be expressed by having an affair, a "nervous breakdown," a severe depression, an immobilization of a person's coping abilities, an avoiding of intimacy for fear of losing self-control, and on and on.

The alternative to keeping rage under cover is not absence of control. You can't just allow your anger and hostility to continually boil over. If you are at the simmering, bubbling-over stage constantly, you need professional help in a hurry. Constant anger and hostility toward each other indicates that the basic needs of the partners in the marriage relationship are not being met. Unsatisfied needs damage the self-image and this frustration leads to hurting each other, which in turn adds guilt to the already critical situation. There are times when it is best to temporarily swallow hurt and anger to avoid a quarrel—for example, if one spouse is going through a time of particular tension or if there are children, in-laws, or friends present.

Some marriages seem to be a constant battleground.

Usually the function of this hostility is to allow a touching without intimacy. If a partner feels overwhelmed or engulfed by the mate, he may panic and try to salvage his identity and autonomy by means of hostile attack. Often, if intimacy threatens to develop, one or the other will pick a fight to gain distance and also to sharpen the sense of identity. This can be done in such a way as to make the one attacking seem to be the innocent victim and thus provide an excuse for not having sex or relating in other ways and also making one person seem responsible for the rift. Hostility is created by people who desperately desire intimacy but constantly sabotage the opportunities.

There are many ways this type of hostility is expressed. (1) The sarcasm of the hot retort uses the tongue as a knife to cut to the soul of the other person. With practice, the tongue is sharpened to the degree that it doesn't just wound; it kills. (2) Sulking is indeed hard to deal with. The person retreats into silence and sullenness. If the other (nonsulker) is trained by the one who sulks long enough, he learns to agree with or flatter to draw the sulking one out. It may not be worth the effort. (3) Cold hostility, the deep-freeze treatment, is very serious as the person doing the freezing refuses to communicate at all. It may be used as punishment for some real or imagined wrong. When one partner has been kept in the freezer long enough, he is supposed to emerge, having benefited by the treatment. This treatment will quickly drain the love out of a marriage. (4) The wounded martyr requires careful handling because he is very tender. "Don't worry about me; I'll be all right." Poor dear. (5) Self-righteous people are so good. They never make mistakes; they know how everything should be run from heaven on down. You don't even have to ask; they will tell you, demonstrating freely. They have a solemn responsibility to point out the flaws of others (especially their mate and children, for starters).

All of these are hard to recognize in ourselves. We see how other people fit these roles. "I am different. My complaints are real; my hurt feelings are justified; I am the innocent party!" Married people have the wonderful possibility of having the understanding and love to deal with these problems in a wholesome way that will allow maximum growth for both.

It is important to learn to deal with negative feelings creatively. If you can deal with resentments openly within the bounds of your love and respect for each other and without attacking the other's self-esteem, you'll be able to move through the conflict to deeper understanding and intimacy.

A lot of marital fighting or disagreement stems from "displaced" anger or resentments. You have to learn to listen and look for this. Long-suppressed anger is likely to burst out at an inappropriate time and place or over something totally unrelated to the real issue. "She got furious at me over nothing" is not an unusual statement for counselors to hear. For example: (1) Husband berates wife for a half-hour in car because she signaled right and turned left. The real reason for his anger was his building resentment over her attitude about sex. (2) Husband "loses interest" in sex because he is angered by his wife's attitude toward his mother. (3) Wife belittles husband's accomplishments because she resents his stinginess.

We fear expressing anger because we're taught that it is wrong, even sinful, and we're afraid of the "wrath of God." Isn't that interesting? We cover our hostility, all the while getting more and more angry at both God and our spouses and all others around us. We can handle knowing about God's anger because we trust him, knowing that he is just and fair and not vindictive. We should strive to imitate him when expressing anger. Behave in a trustworthy way in expressing your anger. Here are some guidelines to fighting fairly and constructive quarreling, taken from observations of a number of family counselors:

a.  Be willing to listen as well as to talk. Listen to the other person's point of view even if it does not make sense to you at the moment. Learn to express yourself in as calm a way as possible.

b.  Timing can be a major factor in a marital argument. Probably the worst times for fights are at the end of an exhausting day, bedtime, and mealtime. "Right now" is probably the worst possible time for settling an argument. A head-on collision is almost inevitable. A postponement allows tempers to cool and gives both persons a chance to look over the situation.

c.  Don't name-call, and don't criticize your spouse for losing a job when you are arguing about something entirely different. This is a deliberate attempt to wound for the sake of wounding.

d.  Don't rake up old scores and old arguments. Stick to the subject. References to other members of the family or "Why do you always . . . ?" damages the chances of resolving a dispute.

e.  Withdrawing, or the silent treatment, diminishes the possibility of compromise and allows misunderstandings to accumulate.

f.  One should never threaten to leave, to divorce, to go home to Mother, or to commit suicide.

g.  It isn't fair to involve other people as allies or "go-betweens."

h.  Never resort to physical violence. Physical fights occur in the middle and upper classes, as well as in the lower classes. Men are more inclined to slap and hit, while women prefer to throw, scratch, bite, and kick.

i.  Tears can evoke compassion and also provoke anger. Tears are a form of manipulation.

j.  When emotions threaten to get out of control, or if the dispute deteriorates into name-calling or physical abuse, call a truce. This may put the immediate cause of the quarrel into a more sensible perspective. It may also call for the truce to hold until morning if it can't be resolved before you go to bed.

How do you end a quarrel? And what about unresolvable

fights? Somehow one must be able to make clear what is hurting him, and the other should make every effort to understand. It is very good if a quarrel can be ended by reaching a solution that is agreeable to both and possibly better than they had achieved before.

1. Sometimes one gives in to the wishes of the other. If this becomes the usual and only way to resolve the quarreling, it is because one is overwhelming the other, beating him into line.

2. Compromise (with good grace) is healthy if it leads to motivating concessions in the future from both parties.

3. End with some evidence of fondness, reassurance that no permanent damage has been done. If you can dissolve anger with warmth, you are saying to each other that life is still there.

4. Arguments are often followed by lovemaking. If this becomes a pattern, it may mean that sex is used to cover fears aroused rather than solving the points involved. Physical lovemaking must be mutually desired after an argument, or it becomes another weapon. Some couples may find lovemaking a satisfying way to end a quarrel, but others may need to cool off first.

5. If the disputed points cannot be resolved, there may be an agreement to disagree and work on a viable alternative. Make allowances for the fact that you might not ever totally agree on certain things, but the one to whom it matters least will make concessions. One spouse should not always be the one to concede. This is unhealthy. Perhaps a sincere "I'll try to handle it better next time" is sufficient to be healing. Actually "next time" may produce the same results, but at least one acknowledges the need to work on a situation.

Every conflict, every quarrel is a matter of one person's will coming into conflict with another person's will. Marriage provides the most opportunities for this to occur. It is worth it to receive the potentials of a loving relationship. Marital quarrels must be fought in the context of affection with the aim of *healing*, not hurting.

It has been said that every marital quarrel is, in a sense, an emotional separation. Every fight is a declaration that we are not appendages of each other. A fight may fill one with a heady freedom and a frightening loneliness. But once ended, we are again sure that it is better to be with our spouse than to be separated. No marriage is compatible all the time. It is remarkable when it is compatible most of the time. This means that the couple has worked out an arrangement where creative interchange can take place and destruction can be kept at a minimum. Marriage has to be kept in good repair. Settle little differences before they get to be big ones. Find a time to be together, really together, listening and talking. Make special times for each other. Speak openly and honestly and freely about real things.

### Grace and Forgiveness—The Miracle

Romans 3:23 teaches us that "All have sinned, and come short of the glory of God" (KJV). None of us can claim to be perfect. Not a day goes by but that we need to ask for forgiveness. Many times we feel very self-righteous and good. After all, we don't commit murder, steal, or cheat, so why should we ask for forgiveness?

The common denominator of each of us in this group is the fact that we have accepted Christ as our personal Savior. Only as we experience the Father's loving forgiveness can we even begin to understand about grace and forgiveness. Sometimes a person is so burdened with his own sinfulness and guilt that he believes that he cannot be forgiven. If you ever feel so bad about yourself, remember that there is never anything you can do that is so bad that God cannot forgive you and wipe the slate clean. He doesn't demand that we grovel, only that we truly are repentant and ask help to be better.

After you have asked forgiveness from God, you must forgive yourself. You don't need to carry the burden any longer. When God takes sin and guilt away, he takes it so far away that it cannot be found—it is forgotten. God provides grace (forgiveness and acceptance) for us, his children. Jesus teaches that in order to receive forgiveness we must be forgiving. This is crucial to the Christian life. A forgiving spirit is to be sought constantly. It is an asset in every area of life.

Repentance and faith in God are crucial to family life. Repentance is a changed attitude, and faith is a positive response to one who is trustworthy (Acts 2:21). Punishment does not bring repentance; love brings change. Love and understanding create the environment for repentance and faith. We are able to remove our masks and not fear rejection. True repentance on the part of the one who needs forgiveness is absolutely essential for forgiveness to be extended.

Have you ever heard anyone say, "I have never had to ask forgiveness from anyone"? You know that person has no deep interpersonal relationships. We are all capable of hurting someone and of being hurt. That is part of receiving and giving friendship—we are vulnerable, open to being hurt and giving hurt.

Forgiveness is a miracle. Forgiveness means that whatever has occurred to hurt will not separate us. The band of love is stronger than whatever separating power would come between us. We experience this miracle of forgiveness as children of God. He redeems us, makes us new and clean and free. Because we are redeemed and forgiven through grace, we must also forgive in the same spirit. What we have experienced in forgiveness immediately demands to become effective in our relationship to others. (a) God is generous; we must be generous. (b) God does not store up bitterness and spite against us; we must not store up bitterness and spite against our fellowman.

Forgiveness is the sole possibility of our escaping the swelling avalanche of guilt and retaliation. We are echoes either of bitterness or of forgiveness. We exhibit qualities of meanness and cheating or of forgiving, creative love. When we receive God's forgiveness, we become loving, forgiving, creative, and positive persons, capable of blessing instead of cursing.

Reconciliation is also a miracle. It means more than the ceasing of hostility. It means that forgiveness and restoration have taken place. It is the miracle of love, soaking up and blotting out hatred, fear, and distrust. Deep trouble and excruciating pain require agonizing work to repair. We put off taking care of these deep wounds till we've almost bled to death. Little hurts and disagreements left unresolved tend to grow in importance. We tend to put these off because we will have to face up to the fact that someone is at fault and changes will have to be made. We resist making changes, especially concerning personal habits and attitudes.

There are at least four important elements in making reconciliation possible:

1. A willingness to discover the problem. This is a major step when both husband and wife are able to do that.
2. A third party may be needed to be a sounding board. A counselor (or someone in that category) is useful because the husband and wife can say to him what they, at this point, cannot say to each other. There is no stigma attached to seeking help in these matters.
3. Christians have forgiveness available in Jesus Christ. The strongest power in the world is ready for use in the Christian family. As Christians we have accepted the gift of forgiveness, but we hesitate to extend this same gift to others. We need the gift of forgiveness often, and we must give this gift generously.
4. What you have said or done does matter and cannot be unsaid or undone. What you have said or done can be soaked up by the compassion of the heavenly Father, and you yourself will continue to be loved. This priceless gift is offered by husbands and wives to one another.

Accepting love means that you take the other person just as he is. The proclamation of Jesus Christ is about the love of God, which is all-inclusive and unconditional. In the parable of the prodigal son, the father did not make the repentance of his son a condition of forgiveness. Forgiveness came spontaneously from the father's heart because it had never been absent from it. God loves us unconditionally; and because of the power of his love for us, we can in turn love others. God loves and forgives; he shows us how we are to do this. We cannot claim to love without reservation as God does. He offers us this reconciliation in Christ. This frees us from the burden of guilt, transforms us, and allows us to love and affirm others. If we withhold this healing love, we become like the elder brother in the prodigal son parable, standing aloof and excluding ourselves from joy. In forgiveness we extend our love to the one who has violated it. To face ourselves and each other honestly and to accept and forgive can clear the way for new marital interaction and allow spouses to relate person to person.

Perhaps the most difficult love and forgiveness to achieve is toward in-laws and ex-spouses. You marry not just your spouse, but also his family, traditions, and loving patterns. Each person brings to the marriage all the feelings you have about your own parents. Mother-in-law jokes are a great mask for covering up real problems, hurts, and pain in the extended family area. In a survey taken in the early 70s in-law problems were the main source of tension in one out of every four cases of marital problems.

General interference and criticism over money, work, sex, religion, child rearing, and homemaking are the usual situations. These differences are manageable when they can be openly discussed (between children and parents), solved by compromise, rejected, or even quietly ignored. The real clashes are a deeper problem—the unresolved feeling a spouse has toward his parents and his past. Unconsciously a man tries to imitate his father and the woman her mother, even while vehemently denying this fact. Or one's background may have been so unpleasant that he may try to create a different image in his own home and have a problem managing this. Marriage forces a person to face his own unconscious feelings about his parents and his past. When we see reflections of parents in our spouses that we don't like we build up resentment toward the offending in-law. This can grow by leaps and bounds if there is no basis for friendship or communication with this person.

Too often, parents think that no one is good enough for their son or daughter. There may have been strenuous opposition to the marriage either openly or subtly. Whichever, there will be hurt feelings that only time and a forgiving spirit can overcome. This happens both with parents concerning son and parents concerning daughter. Those who have accepting, gracious in-laws do not know how much they have to be grateful for. That acceptance as part of the family is the most wonderful wedding gift ever given or received— and it must be received in a loving spirit.

Whatever the hurts or the problems you have with in-laws, begin to pray for strength and graciousness to forgive and not hold a grudge. Work on yourself with God's help to have a kind and understanding spirit. Your spouse owes you the courtesy of hearing your hurts, of being open-minded and supportive. Your first responsibility now is to each other. Seek outside help if you cannot discuss your in-law situation to the satisfaction of both of you.

When two people have lived together a period of time, they have become part of each other. Even those who fight all the time or have an armed truce cannot be completely indifferent to each other. When one or the other or both decide to leave the relationship, it is a wrenching, difficult situation. It is natural to find places to dump anger and frustration when divorce takes place. Resentment and unresolved anger and hurt go on for years after the marriage has been dissolved. These keep coming up in the form of children, property, mutual friends, and old family ties. Without one's finally working through the anger and working toward a forgiving spirit, the bitterness will be forever present. It will make life miserable for you and all around you. Forgiveness of this sort comes slowly and painfully, but it can be done.

You will need help to work it out. Don't let it fester and stay just under the surface to keep you miserable. Clean the wound and get well. Let healing come through forgiveness. The scar will remain, but it will fade with time if you allow it to. A forgiving spirit is worth working on. "Forgive us as we are forgiven."

## Work Space

1. What do you fuss (argue) about most? Is it money, in-laws, children? Write down your answers individually; then compare with your spouse's.

2. Honestly talk to your spouse about areas of conflict. If you are covering something over, now is the time to tell your spouse about it. Talk about better ways to take care of conflict than you are now doing.

3. a. There are some very lively ghosts around in many marriages in the form of former spouses. We are prisoners of the past in many respects. Cutting ties to past relationships and learning to live in present relationships is vital to the health of your marriage. Discuss ways to handle anger, confusion, apprehension over ex-spouses. Realistically, give ways of coping with hurts that continually spring up over this.

   b. Are you able to understand or at least be open-minded to your spouse's feelings about your children? Can you help in dealing with jealousy on both sides? Discuss this in the group.

Divide into three groups, discuss one problem, and report to large group.

**Problem 1.** Bob has always been a quiet man who seemed to love his wife and family. Mary had not had much difficulty pleasing him with good meals and pleasant surroundings. He worked late during certain busy times of the year, but always called and told Mary he'd not be home for dinner. Then Mary's mother became sick in a distant city and she had to go to take care of her. She was gone longer than she anticipated, but each time she called Bob was understanding and didn't push her to come home. When her mother recovered sufficiently for her to leave, Mary came home. When Bob met her at the airport, she sensed something was wrong. She pressed him and he told her how one of the office secretaries had fixed dinner for him, occasionally at first, then regularly. Since he was lonesome, they had become quite fond of each other. But he loved Mary and begged her to forgive him.

Can Mary forgive him? Without forever bringing this up? What about the secretary friend—can she forgive her? How will they work this out? Is Mary also at fault?

**Problem 2.**　　When Dan married Joyce his parents were violently opposed to the marriage. They felt that Joyce was not the girl for their son and criticized her endlessly. Both mother and father were vicious in their criticism. Joyce knew and heard all this, but felt that this would all change once they married. However, it has not changed much except that the opposition has been covered slightly. Joyce feels justified in thinking that they want the marriage to fail. True, they are doing all they can to undermine the marriage. Dan thinks Joyce is overreacting. Now that there is a grandchild, the tension is building in another area—child rearing. Joyce is a poor mother, etc., to hear the parents. Poor Dan, having to live in such a dirty house, no homemade bread, and now the baby isn't being reared to "our standards."

Can Joyce ever forgive her in-laws? Can she forgive Dan for allowing his parents to continue to harass them? How can this be solved in a forgiving way?

**Problem 3.** Tom decided that after ten years of marriage, he was tired of being stuck with one woman and three hyperactive children (his words). He had found that Sue did not like his new lifestyle—a bachelor pad and a stream of pretty girls. She wouldn't let him come home for a night or two a week without screaming at him for being a scoundrel. So they divorced. She had trouble getting child support from him; and after she remarried, he sent money only sporadically. It was difficult for Sue because her new husband was also divorced, but paid his obligations to his children regularly (as Sue wanted him to). It was embarrassing to her to know that her new husband was having to support two families.

The sources of unresolved anger and resentment abound in this illustration. Point them out. Can forgiveness happen here? Can a miracle of grace and forgiveness come about?

# 8. Becoming One Flesh

*Bible Passages:*     Genesis 2:24; Proverbs 30:18-19;
                      Matthew 19:6; 1 Corinthians 7:3-5; Mark
                      12:28-32; Psalm 139:23-24; 25:4-5

*T*he Christian marriage is symbolized by the wedding
band—a perfect, never-ending circle representing a
never-ending relationship. The couple, committed to
each other, continuously interact within this circle. There is
constant ebb and flow between the two. When one is dominant, the other is recessive and vice versa.

A mental, emotional, and spiritual unit must be created
because only this type of love can raise this expression above
the physical and make it a unique expression of man and
woman as "one flesh." The richness or poverty of a couple's
sexual experience largely depends on the total communication and trust of the two. Books abound on techniques in
lovemaking. However, all knowledge and technique in this
intimate encounter is superficial and incomplete unless it is
based on a deep mutual love, care, trust, and readiness to
collaborate and care for each other in the tenderness of
everyday life. "They shall become one flesh" symbolically
suggests the living experience of two harmonious people in
communion.

Sex is not a four-letter word. Sex and love may not be
substituted for one another. Many times during the dating
years people confuse the desire for sex with love, and there
is a big difference. We have talked about the fact that we
bring to the marriage the culmination of our experience in
every area. Sex is no exception. This is a fact we cannot
ignore. I know that I am speaking to Christians, but we must
face reality. For whatever reason, in many cases one or both

spouses come to marriage having had premarital sexual experience. This needs to be spoken to in several ways.

First, in case someone reads this who is not yet married, we need to say very clearly that sexual intercourse before marriage is wrong in the eyes of God. And, contrary to popular modern sex mythology, it does not do anything to help your adjustment in marriage; in fact, it may well be detrimental.

Second, it can be well documented by Christian counselors and social workers that sex out of marriage has a devastating effect on the self-respect of the individual, though he may deny it.

Third, sex out of marriage, promiscuity, and concurrent polygamy all make sex an experience devoid of deep feeling and tenderness. People who have these kinds of "backseat, thirty-minute cheap motel" experiences eventually despair of deep intimacy and understanding. If you take sex lightly before marriage and it doesn't mean much to you except conquest or satisfying curiosity, you'll find that it is difficult to develop any other kind of response. It becomes a pattern of behavior that is not appropriate to marriage and that is all but impossible to change.

Fourth, it is not fair to your mate to bring a load of emotional garbage to a new relationship that you intend to make meaningful. If you are in this category, you must ask God to forgive you; you must forgive yourself and turn your back on past experiences which could emotionally damage your marriage. This applies to both men and women. Too often we assume that because women become unwed mothers or suffer an abortion or miscarriage, the man has no feeling. It affects both and leaves emotional scars. If you have trouble forgiving yourself and getting that part of your life behind you, get professional help right away.

Fifth, in spite of modern birth control, scientific knowledge, and all the variations of penicillin, there are new strains of venereal disease that defy treatment. They are brought under control only to flare up again and again. Promiscuity before marriage can ruin your chances for normal sexual adjustment because of disease. Infidelity can bring disaster into a marriage. It is not right to expose your mate to this very real possibility. Yes, there are church members, Christians, who are dealing with these devastating problems.

If you have been married before, we make these suggestions:

1. We assume, hopefully, that you have allowed ample time for wounds and hurts to sufficiently heal so that you can enter a new relationship without fear of reviving some old pains.

2. Check on your self-esteem. Be sure that you are able to love yourself and relate to your new spouse in a mature way.

3. Do each other the favor of making every effort to really begin anew in this relationship and not make your spouse "pay" for old resentments. You may think that your former problems were in areas other than sex, but all phases of life come to focus in this important expression of love.

4. One or both of you may have difficulty in being able to trust your spouse because you were so crushed by previous experience. Express this to one another if it is true; understand how deep the problem is; and be extra aware of this area of sensitivity. It can be overcome with work on both sides.

5. A widow or widower may have so idolized the dead spouse that no one is good enough to compare with him or take his place. We very kindly have the tendency to make the dead "perfect" when in actuality he was not so. No one is to "take the place of" anyone. If this is a problem go to a counselor quickly and get your head on straight. Proper respect is certainly desired, but morbid remembering will kill your new relationship. This sounds harsh, but you must face facts. The funeral serves a real purpose. It is a ceremony for burial and allows grief to be expressed. We don't have that privilege for a dead marriage that ends.

6. New love, a new mate—whether you are widowed or divorced, expect this to be a beautiful new relationship. Allow it to grow and blossom with all the attention you can give it.

The need for sexual harmony in marriage is of great importance to the happiness of the couple. Often this is the first major adjustment that couples have to face, and it is important to really work at understanding each other in this area. Serious frustration and hurt feelings regarding sex are hard to overcome and can destroy feelings of warmth and tenderness for each other. Sex can be the utmost of being together, or it can be agonizing and wanting, hurting and being hurt. Sex can be warm and generous or stingy and selfish.

There are times in every marriage when sex does not go well. There are many reasons for this.

1. Lack of knowledge and understanding may enhance any problem. There are too many good doctors and books to allow this to continue to be a hindrance.
2. Guilt and fear can cause lack of interest and responsiveness in both men and women. Childhood inhibitions cloud the picture. Ghosts of the past may parade through the bedroom. One may have to learn to say yes to sexual pleasure. This will take counseling and an understanding mate.
3. A man or woman may have fears about whether or not the sexual organs are adequate or will perform correctly. Also, fear of pregnancy may be a real problem. All these can be helped with counseling from a good physician.
4. Sometimes one or both partners may be too exhausted to respond satisfactorily. It is important to reduce the "demand quality" of sex. Accept the fact that your sex life will have variations; do not feel that you have to prove your masculinity or femininity by a successful performance. Relax and enjoy lovemaking.
5. Overwork, lack of appropriate time together, lack of

privacy, and lack of energy may diminish sexual interest. Be aware of these problems and change the external factor (get household help, find ways of getting rest, etc.).

6. Unexpressed hostility can cause poor sexual relations. Learn to express and resolve anger rather than letting it accumulate.

7. Infidelity naturally creates barriers in the marital relationship. Fidelity is essential to a growing relationship and to a good sexual adjustment.

Sexual problems, as a rule, are not problems of sex but of the relationship between the couple or emotional problems. The expectations of one may not be understood by the other, or one may be more desirous of sex than the other. Preconceived ideas about what is "normal" must be removed; and realistic, reasonable ideas satisfying to both should be substituted. Both need to be aware of the total picture. Time, patience, and understanding are necessary so that neither one will feel like a failure. There is no "correct" or "proper" way to "perform" sexual union. The goal is to meet the sexual needs of each other in mutual love. This requires continual work and mutual trust. Be free to experiment and to talk about feelings and responses. He cannot be assumed to know what you are experiencing if you don't tell him in the spirit of love and caring (not a put-down or attack on the person).

There is no room in marriage for infidelity. It will not only kill the marriage, but it will also destroy the self-esteem of the offended spouse and cause emotional problems for the two offending persons. Any type of involvement that threatens the mate threatens the marriage. Remember that what begins as a platonic friendship often develops and becomes sexual. Then the mate involved has to determine who he is going to hurt— the mate to whom he has committed himself before God or the "friend" with whom he can "communicate." Try putting at least the same amount of effort into understanding and communicating with your spouse as with your friend. Give him a chance; get to know your spouse.

Each person must learn to deal with jealousy. Some jealousy is normal and good; it indicates caring. Inordinate jealousy is an evidence of lack of self-esteem and of deeper emotional problems. Jealousy can kill a marriage. This works both ways. The level of trust determines what is threatening to each other. Be open and communicate about this and get professional help if you need to before the marriage dies or one mate gets pushed too far.

Infidelity is usually thought of as an opposite-sex affiliation. We are seeing more and more cases of a spouse leaving for another of his own sex. This is just as destructive as opposite-sex infidelity. There is emotional instability and mental disturbance in both types of infidelity if not checked and dealt with immediately.

One who cannot be faithful and realizes this flaw before marriage should not inflict this pain and problem on a marriage. Being married will not cure an emotional instability problem. It takes two mature, healthy-minded persons to grow a beautiful relationship in marriage.

The words of the marriage ceremony—to love, honor, and cherish—contain an implicit truth vital to the marriage relationship. A couple cannot really love deeply unless they also appreciate, respect, nurture, and hold each other dear. The quality and value of the whole relationship drastically affects the meaning and satisfaction derived from sexual intercourse. In a healthy marriage, sexual feelings are intertwined with everything that goes on in the relationship. Sex is affirmed and enjoyed and gives a good relationship warmth and joy. It is an integral part of the total marriage and reflects the health or sickness of this relationship. In marriage, our sexual response to our mate is an emotional and spiritual experience. Sex is communion, giving and receiving. Genuine love of husband and wife brings the impulse toward intimacy of touch and feeling and fulfillment of desire. Human beings make love face to face with all the vulnerable areas of the body exposed. Because of this intimacy, this exposure to each other, there is the greatest need to give each a sense of security in being totally loved, honored, and cherished. There is no room in any marriage for infidelity. Each one should have the inner feeling of stability and safety in this relationship, knowing that he is accepted, wanted, and belongs. Trust is essential in a good, rewarding sexual relationship in marriage.

Sex is misused, abused, when used as a weapon. When seen as a means of bolstering one's own ego rather than as a giving and loving act, sex is used as a tool and the act becomes one of hostility. Withholding sex and/or insisting on sexual intercourse is a self-centered way of dealing with problems that are too deep-seated and painful to acknowledge. Counselors report that this abuse of sex is not unusual. Sex is a battle for many couples, and they fight to the death for control. Only a few ways of doing this are:

a. Withhold sex to gain a material objective. (He wants sex; she wants a fur coat. She extracts the promise before sleeping with him.) Sex may be the "rate of exchange" and sometimes the rate of no exchange.

b. A woman may refuse to respond or allow herself to become aroused to punish him or to degrade him.

c. Sex may be the key to winning or losing an argument. Or some may demand sex as a way of reconciliation after a quarrel.

d. Infidelity is a weapon—making sure the spouse learns about it—of hurt and retaliation.

## Some Ways of Strengthening Intimacy

• Choose to sit close together in a restaurant, or at an event where each has mingled with friends; at dinner time search each other out and sit together.

• A fond glance, a tender touch, a note left where it will be found.

• An appropriate word of support, a nod or wink across the room.

• Preparing a favorite dish; remembering to carry out the trash.

- Being aware of particular days when workload is unusually heavy and help with dinner or other chores.
- Really listen—be present with your mind and body—give your presence.
- Check out meanings if you aren't sure—"Is this what you are saying?"
- Care about what the other is saying or feeling—care enough to comment or provide some sort of comfort.
- Listen for your own words of criticism and learn a better way to let your spouse know your feelings. Learn to be "nonattacking."
- Bring your spouse a surprise occasionally.
- Receive the surprise happily and graciously.
- Learn about coded messages and how to decipher them. Coded messages can be both verbal and nonverbal.
- Learn to use conflict and unhappiness (which are bound to occur in any close relationship) as a stepping-stone to greater intimacy. Learn to resolve differences by focusing on one issue at a time, and check out meanings calmly.
- Never assume that your spouse "knows" you love him. Find ways to show and tell.
- Look in his eyes and say his name—again and again—until he is affirmed. Then switch roles.
- Check out ambiguous nonverbal messages to help sex be mutually satisfying.
- There is no ideal sexual relationship. Each couple should find the unique pattern which is most fulfilling to both. Realize that this will surely change through the years.
- Cultivate the art of lovemaking. Discover what encourages spontaneity and playfulness.
- Create the needed atmosphere to allow the most pleasure and response for both.
- Set aside regular times to be together—protect that time from encroachment (work, children, friends, etc.). Take a walk, talk, listen to music, eat by candlelight, sit by an open fire, read a good book together, get a babysitter and be away from the children, forget that you are an adult

and a parent—whatever is relaxing and enjoyable to both of you.

- Newlyweds should begin to build memories. Older marrieds sometimes find new closeness by looking through old photograph albums together, reading old letters, revisiting places from courtship or early marriage days.
- Continue to grow intellectually. Be open to change. Risk moving on to newer levels of maturity and learning. Don't solidify patterns into a rigid form.
- Be willing to live in the present; don't hang on to the past. Don't grieve over looking your age. Most people (men and women) can look more beautiful/handsome as they get older if they take care of themselves.
- Share the beauty of nature, the timeless. Put yourselves in places where the wonders of nature can be enjoyed.
- Delight in the antics of your child. Remember the union with yourselves and God that created him. An adopted child is a special gift. Join together in rearing your children.
- Explore the endless possibilities of missionary service— career or short-term. Helping others and working in concert with others will help give a wider vision and strengthen both family and spiritual ties.
- Agree on your family responsibility to give money, time, and talent to your church. This is a rewarding spiritual experience.
- Release yourself to grow spiritually. Religion is more than moralism (thou shalt not). Get out of the trivia stage of spiritual growth.
- Release yourselves to growth: intimate, loving, caring growth, both horizontally and vertically.
- Don't take yourself too seriously—be able to laugh at yourself. Keep and enhance your sense of humor.

## Work Space

1.  What were the factors influencing you in your mate selection?
    a.

    b.

    c.

    d.

2.  Is there a gap between what you expected and what you experience in the sexual relationship of marriage?
    a.  If yes, to what do you attribute this?

    b.  How can you help correct this?

3.  Are you aware of the things that please your spouse? Make an effort to discuss the things that each of you enjoys most when you make love. What would make it better?

4.  Do you find it difficult to talk about sex—your sex life as a couple?
5.  Do you use every opportunity to make your mate feel loved and appreciated?
6.  Do you enjoy just being with each other?
7.  Are you stingy with your verbal and physical expressions of love?
8.  Do you see growing in sexual intimacy and pleasure as a part of improving the quality of your marriage as a whole?
9.  Make an effort to say and do the things which affirm your mate's sexuality but which you may tend to neglect. Write some of these down to help you remember.

## Review

### Self-Esteem

God paid us (mankind) his highest compliment by creating us in his image. We learned in Psalm 139 that God knows everything about us. Each individual has combinations of experience, abilities, capabilities, and spiritual gifts which equip us for living.

Dr. Herb Barks, president of the Baylor School in Chattanooga, Tennessee, has said in a very unique way, "God didn't make any junk!" We need to remember that when we begin to put ourselves down. We need to develop a good self-image, a self-concept that is based on the fact that God so loved the world (meaning each individual) that he gave his Son to set us free and save us from eternal damnation.

1.  List six of your skills and abilities.

    a.

    b.

    c.

    d.

    e.

    f.

2.  What are your strengths? Personality traits?

    a.

    b.

    c.

    d.

    e.

    f.

## Male and Female

Every creature glorifies God by being what it is, by living up to God's idea of it or him/her. We are individually the sum total of our inheritance of genes, environment, and countless other things. We will be changing and growing all of our lives. There are many things in a couple coming together to be married that could separate them, but durability will overcome the uncertainties of life.

The love of husband and wife for each other must be based on the health of each one's self-esteem. Anton T. Boisen, the founder of the modern pastor-care movement in America, has said love between man and woman can be truly happy only when each is a free and autonomous being, dependent not on each other but upon God. When a man's love for a woman is such that he draws not from the common source of strength, but clings to her, he is not worthy of her.

Thinking of your relationship as husband and wife, answer these questions:

1.  Are you uncomfortable when you are separated from your spouse in a gathering? Do you feel that you have to be silent in social groups so that his/her ego will not be damaged? Do you depend on his/her social ability to provide friends for you also?
2.  Are you able to handle situations on your own, make decisions (not the big budget breakers!) competently?
3.  Can you allow each other space to move and grow and then come together, appreciating the resourcefulness and creative ability of each other?

## Understanding Money

The family finances provide the number 1 problem for marriages. Money can become a club for punishment; the way it is handled may be indicative of emotional problems of one or both spouses. Take a hard look at the way you manage your money. Is it an uncomfortable situation? Money can represent love, fear, hate, anger, protection, power, sexual inadequacy, or revenge.

Every couple should have some kind of mutually agreed upon plan for handling finances. A realistic budget worked out by mature individuals with similar spending habits will be flexible and satisfactory to both. More important than the budget itself is the attitude the husband and wife have toward it.

### Relating to Each Other as Husband and Wife

What is a husband? What is a wife? Have you agreed on what kind of marriage you want?

Also review the section in chapter 3 concerning the biblical perspective of equality and submission. Remember that respect and trust are prerequisites for love.

Your marriage will not be like that of any other couple. Your marriage will be unique; never try to make it fit a mold that seems to work for someone else. Marriage is a growing process and should never be finished "till death do you part."

### Becoming One Flesh

To love, honor, and cherish indicates a beautiful truth that is vital in any marriage relationship. A couple cannot really love deeply unless they also appreciate, respect, nurture, and hold each other dear. The quality of the whole relationship drastically affects the meaning and satisfaction derived from sexual intercourse. Fidelity in marriage is absolutely necessary if you wish a beautiful, open communion—if you really want to understand your spouse and, in turn, be understood.

Be sure to complete number 9 on the work space for chapter 8.

# Part III
# Religion and Marriage

# 9. *Learn to Pray and Seek God's Will*

*Bible Passages:*   Psalm 127:1; 107:27-28; 8:3-4; Ruth
1:15-17; Daniel 6:10; Jonah 2:7;
Hebrews 4:15-16; John 17:20-23; Luke
11:1-4; Matthew 10:29-31; Romans
8:28; Matthew 7:11; John 4:10

*P*erhaps your family never hears you utter any words in
prayer except a childish, memorized couplet at mealtime or another time. Could it be that you only call
God's name when you are in pain (hit your thumb with a
hammer) or in a difficult situation (automobile accident; grave
illness)? This puts the use of prayer in the category of spas-
modic crying in a time of crisis or at least when we want him
to do something special for us. This misuse of prayer negates
our use of the power of God to guide our lives in every way.
It is a selfishness that few human beings overcome for any
extended period of time. We forget God until we need him
for our benefit. God is more than a power to call in occasionally to help with some immovable obstacle (whatever its
form) that looms in our lives. We limit God's power in us and
in the world when we allow our praying to become only like
a child's begging.

The psalmist prayed in all circumstances, and we can
learn from these prayers of praise, of anger and rebellion, and
of agony and thankfulness. This means that we can talk to
God anytime, anywhere, about anything. As we said earlier,
in the fullest expression of intimacy there is not only the horizontal dimension but also a vertical dimension. This includes
not only spiritual feeding from your church relationship, but

the shared commitment to spiritual growth. The life of the spirit is so deeply personal that moments of sharing on this level are very precious and tender.

Intimacy on the horizontal level and intimacy on the vertical level reinforce and complement each other. The ability to establish and nurture intimate relationships and the ability to commune with God and appreciate nature are closely related.

Here again is the importance of trust. When one trusts God, he can more easily trust his spouse. A source of regular spiritual trust renewal also provides a basis for strength in human trust relationships.

Again, we underline the need for self-esteem to cultivate an intimate relationship. This comes from knowing that one is accepted and related to the Creator of the universe.

Shared religion is a strengthening agent in marriage. This is upheld by numerous studies which show that there is great correlation between church attendance and greater marital stability. Worship is nurturing and trust restoring with the church family. These relationships undergird the values of the family.

A husband and wife who have mixed religious backgrounds face a challenge that can be devastating if not handled properly.

a.   They should try to communicate in order to understand and come to a compromise on such matters as in which tradition the children will be reared.

b.   They need to find a common ground, if possible. Religion and worship is a celebration. It is a good thing to celebrate together.

c.   They must work it out—ignoring it won't make it go away.

Religious difference may be a cover for psychological problems. Sometimes superreligious people suddenly react and strange behavior may result. For example: (1) The husband and wife who play the dominant (husband/submissive wife) game in the name of religion. After ten years, she rebels and leaves husband and children to "discover herself." (2) Or the husband who doesn't meet his wife's expectations in his spiritual development and she continually reminds him of this. One day he rebels and refuses to participate in church activities at all; or he has a spiritual awakening and revival and she can't handle this new dimension in him. She withdraws from him and the church.

Truly religious, spiritual people are not sad, pessimistic, boring people. They are joyous, exciting, adventurous, and courageous, with an ability springing from an inward spiritual source for plowing through troubled times without going to pieces and tearing their world apart. The ability to face crisis times depends on spiritual resources.

It is really important to bring faith and marital life together because faith in God as Father brings a transforming power and understanding to allow total unity in the marriage relationship. Paul Tournier has suggested that we have silent moments alone with God to renew our souls and then we can overcome the holding back of the soul that would jeopardize marital oneness. Our relationship with the heavenly Father allows a more wonderful marriage and, through each other, allows us to experience God himself.

This paragraph is added as an afterthought; yet the more I think about it, the more I am convinced that this is a hidden but real problem to some couples. Religion is an area where a couple will quite often fall back on their own family traditions. For example, a husband may discover that, in his eyes, his wife is not as "godly" as he remembers his mother being. Never mind that he can't be specific or that he unrealistically assumed all along that his mother's faith would get him to heaven. Now he tries to put that burden on his wife. It is time for him to develop his own relationship with God, the Father, through Christ. Or a wife remembers fondly that her father always prayed in church, was in places of leadership, seemed to be "in charge" of all situations, and made all decisions (religious or not). If she discovers that her husband isn't ready for such a forceful role, she becomes disenchanted and begins to figure out how to make him like her father. We forget that our own parents were once young and insecure and had to find their own ways. Our memory of them begins after they had family responsibilities to deal with and time to mature.

You can't shame a person or in any other way make him into your ideal in any area. The best thing to do is to step back and see the good qualities in your spouse. Do your best to allow this person to grow and mature into what God wants for him, not what you want. You'll be surprised at the new joy and appreciation you'll develop in each other. Do you breathe a prayer often during the day for your spouse? It is wonderful and brings a new level of intimacy to know that no matter how far away or how close my spouse is, he will be praying for me many times during the day, and I for him.

There is another pitfall that I hate to see couples fall into. It is really pushed on us by those who have to structure everything tightly and give little room for allowing God to work any other way. A phrase I've heard more and more lately is usually from a young wife who mourns: "I have to wear the spiritual pants in my family." I really dislike that term. We are all stripped bare before God. People, both men and women, have different gifts, different capabilities, and grow at varying rates in their religious faith and commitment. We often get tired of carrying the burden of being the strong one, or the religious one, or the breadwinner, or the parent always on call. The ideal for your family may be a softening of demands on each other and allowing God to mature us individually as he sees fit. In the meantime either husband or wife must keep the family unit in a pattern of spiritual growth both in the home and in relation to your church. Never cease to pray for each other.

There are certain basic things to remember about praying. First of all, the disciples asked Jesus to teach them to pray. Read Luke 11:1-4. It was such a natural thing for Jesus to talk to his Father, his disciples wanted the power and strength he obviously received from this encounter. This means that we are special; only those who are committed can claim the prayer promises of Jesus. The prayer Jesus taught his disciples was a model on which to base our prayers. Jesus covered every need that ever would be. He even made us part of the family of God when he said, "Our Father."

Also, God cares for and is dealing with each one of us. Nothing is too small for our heavenly Father to hear from us. Read Matthew 10:29-31. Even the sparrows are precious to him. Read John 17:20-23 and hear Jesus, in his prayer for intercession for us, saying that God loved them, even as he loved Jesus. I especially like Hebrews 4:15-16, "We may receive mercy, and may find grace to help us in the time of need" (NASB). This is the revelation in Christ of the fact that God, our heavenly Father, cares about you, about me. We can be confident in the reality of praying; it is not just tradition. It seems unbelievable that individuals can be worth so much (Ps. 8:3-4). And he knows us by name!

Think of how we deprive ourselves when we do not pray. Sometimes we tend to think, "Poor God, I haven't talked to him lately!" This is to our detriment when we neglect our relationship with our Father through prayer. It is comparable to the way our relationship as husband and wife can disintegrate when we neglect to keep the lines of communication open. This leads to the conclusion that prayer, in its purest form, is communication with our heavenly Father; it is developing a relationship with God in the midst of whatever life brings.

Prayer is a personal encounter with our heavenly Father. Sometimes we act like our religion and prayer life is so personal that we cannot share even a few of our needs in a normal way. Now you have a partner in that closest sense, one with whom you share your deepest thoughts. The adventure of praying together as husband and wife can be one of your deepest sources of understanding. Of course, you can't share something you don't have. Now is the time to begin this adventure.

We must give God a chance to work his will in and for and through us. He cannot do much for the person with a closed heart and mind. We must give the Father a chance to work his will through us. Prayer is the way to give God an opportunity to do through us what he wants done in his wisdom and love. If you look at history and at the lives of people in relation to the work that is accomplished in the world, you will see that God uses people to build hospitals, schools, churches, bridges, etc. What could a bridge have to do with God's will? In Bangkla, Thailand, near the Cambodian border, a mission hospital could not be built until a road and bridge were built. In areas of the world where the desert is covering more and more of the land mass, our missionaries are working to irrigate and teach farming methods. People are the Christ incarnate (God in the flesh) when his will is worked through their lives.

So where does that leave you and your spouse? Well, for one thing, just because you're married doesn't mean that you stop praying for God's will in your life. Just because you're married doesn't mean that you stop growing as an individual and as a family. It is really more important than ever for your heart to be open to God's desires. Now you have a spouse and perhaps children who are involved.

Many times when couples come to the Foreign Mission Board for appointment as missionaries, their biographies will show that one heard God's missionary call early, perhaps as a teenager, and then felt God definitely leading in marriage toward a person who was not in a religious vocation. They tell how through their prayer and openness to each other and to God their lives worked in this direction. It may have taken a number of years, but God got two instead of one and they grew and matured in the process. This is the way we should always be: open and willing to have God's power and purpose channeled through our lives.

Part of the problem we have as humans is the ever-present desire to dictate what we feel is best, not only for us but for everybody. We say, "If God would only do things my way," instead of standing ready to receive and be made a vehicle for his power to be transmitted. How many times do we pray determined and intent on what we want rather than seeking what God wants? No wonder we are often disappointed that "God didn't hear my prayer," because we pray determined to get what we want, demanding certain things of God. We must learn to pray, listening for what God wants to give us. That could be patience to wait for a blessing we want immediately, or courage to endure a pain we wish to evade, or even leadership in a place of service where we are afraid to venture. Our prayer is a failure when we are determined to have our own way, to change God. Our prayer should be our offering God the opportunity to speak to us, give to us, and work through us, to release our lives to him to work out his purposes. We often set limits on God because we don't want to be disturbed too much. When things are going well for us, we frequently think that we are the power station instead of being the transmitter of unseen resources. When we ask for God's will to be done through us, we have to remember to acknowledge the source of our power and remain in constant contact.

Often in the winter months the mountains of northern Georgia receive an icy covering over every leaf, twig, limb, and wire. The wires that are frozen break off and the power that usually runs through them is immediately broken and it is useless for its purpose—to generate energy to make things work. But be careful of those live wires! They can kill! Aren't we that way? When we are frozen over and broken from the source of power we're useless except that we surely can be harsh and downright cruel when we're separated and unharnessed.

When we pray "Thy will be done," the underlying feeling is sometimes "Thy will be endured" or "Thy will be changed." We are really afraid to allow God to control our lives. We are the losers when this attitude prevails. We have to have receptive hearts before we can receive any of the gifts he has for us. Read Matthew 7:11 and John 4:10. You know very well that you can't give a gift to someone who will not receive it. Parents can offer an education in a fine college to a son or daughter and that is a wonderful gift, but if the child does not accept it, the gift is forever unclaimed.

Sometimes we confuse only the difficult times of agony as being God's will. We suffer because of the consequences of the human dilemma and the fact that we live in an imperfect world. If we pray for God's will to be done, we do not expect to be exempt from trouble, but we can expect to receive strength to face it and defeat it.

One thing we need to remember: we choose a level of life and God has to work with us where we are. He does the best thing possible with the circumstances we give him. We can learn from all situations and raise the level of the quality of life. Don't settle for *good* things; get the *best*.

As you take a quiet time each day this week to search for God's will in your life and for your family, remember these suggestions:

1.  Open your heart and mind to the power of God.
2.  Be willing to use and develop the talents God gave you.
3.  Realize that God can only work with what you give him.
4.  Be patient in working through the obstacles that seem to block the way. Learn what God has to teach you through these circumstances.

## Daily Devotional Guide

Use this as a guide for your private devotional time and also your time with your spouse.

Before you go your separate ways each day, take a moment and pray for your spouse, for his protection and safe return at the end of the workday. Also pray that each of you will be a source of strength for the kingdom of God.

### Sunday

Read Psalm 8. Remember some of the beauties of nature you have experienced in the past week. Remember the happiest time you shared with your spouse during the past week. Write these here.

Pray—Heavenly Father, thank you for the beauties of nature (name some). Help me to be more aware of your gifts. Thank you for (husband/wife—by name). Thank you for bringing us together. In Jesus' name. Amen.

### Monday

Read Matthew 6:25-34; 10:29-31.

We come to God as our heavenly Father. He has such a large family; we have such a large family. Learn to view your associates, friends, and family as God's children, just as you are. Remember that you never have to feel lonely or desolate and no matter what you have done, God loves you. We can never deserve his love.

Write down the names of some people for whom you need to pray. Perhaps you know they are hurting; or perhaps they have hurt you; include your immediate family also.

Pray—Thank you, kind Heavenly Father, for your loving care. I am anxious about (name them: paying bills, people, job, relationships, whatever). Please give me strength and courage and insight in dealing with these concerns. Thank you for knowing about me. Let me be more understanding to those nearest me (name your spouse and children). Help me to be a good member of the family of God. In Jesus' name. Amen.

**Tuesday**
Read Psalm 5:1-3, 11-12.

Make these verses your prayer today. Remember to take refuge in the heavenly Father's love; do not try to control the universe, not even your own little corner of it. Let go and let God work it out.

Pray—Heavenly Father, thank you for hearing my sighs, my groans, as I struggle with living. Morning by morning without end, you hear my cries of distress, of joy. Spread your protection over me, over (spouse), over (children). Let us love you and serve you and mature with each day. Thank you for your sustaining grace. In Jesus' name. Amen.

**Wednesday**
Read James 4:11.

Words used against fellow human beings can be more devastating and painful than actual physical abuse. Be careful of your language. A cutting word can never be recalled. Be a healing child of God.

Pray—Father, help me to be careful not to judge others or speak harsh words that cut and sting. Please help me to learn to be a healing influence at home, at work, and to all with whom I deal. Let me show my love for (spouse). In Jesus' name. Amen.

**Thursday**
Read Ephesians 4:31-32.

Pray—Dear Father, thank you for your words to help me know the way to live. Help me to get rid of the bitterness and rage that keeps returning even after I think it's over. Let kindness and compassion be evident in my life. Help us (you and spouse) to be forgiving toward each other. Let us not hold grudges. Teach us to be open and honest about these problems we have. (Name the problems.) Thank you for your forgiveness to me. In Jesus' name. Amen.

**Friday**

Read John 14:13-14; 15:7.

"Ask anything in my name" is a powerful statement. "If ye abide in me" is the key phrase. Abide means commitment forever. These words are for those who really mean business about doing God's will. Jesus went to Gethsemane for us and he understands all about us. Do not fear to seek God's will. Pray for your marriage and family and for continued openness to God.

**Saturday**

Read 1 Timothy 1:15-17.

Pray—Thank you, Father, that even one as sinful as I am can still claim you as Father. Forgive me for the impatience I have exhibited this week. People just do not react as I think they should! Grant me patience with (name people specifically). Show me how to deal with these situations (name them). Prepare our hearts for the coming day of worship. Bless our church, the staff (name them), my Sunday School teacher (by name), and the class. May we minister to each other and be ready to reach out to others. In Jesus' name. Amen.

## Work Space

Divide into groups—couples separated.
1. Give each one an opportunity to tell briefly how he feels God has led in his life thus far.
2. Do you feel that God is satisfied with where you are in your life now? Do you feel that there will be changes, possibly big ones, in the future? Are you ready to be flexible and open and creative in allowing God to use your life? Are you afraid?

   (Discuss these in the group, giving all an opportunity to express an opinion briefly and then present a composite to the larger group.)
3. Decide on a good time for you to have your family devotionals. Pledge to each other that you will try this plan for at least the next week.
4. Pray for your spouse by name every day.
5. Talk to each other about these things:
   a. What makes life worth living to you?
   b. How you feel and believe about religion.
   c. Have any of the above changed since marriage? Explain.
   d. If you are newly wed, what would you like to make your priorities in the area of values (religious practices)?
   e. If you have been married several years or more, what would you like to see changed in your marriage and family in the areas of values and religious practices?
6. Discuss and take an inventory of all the questions mentioned in the section under group discussion.

   Make these questions a part of your prayer life. Write down things that bother you, things you are thankful for, what frightens you (future, etc.). Pray especially for deepening trust in God to lead your life.

# 10. Learn to Cope with Problems and Trouble

*Bible Passages:*    1 Peter 2:20-21; Matthew 6:25-34;
6:14-15; Psalm 37; 103:13-14; 1
Corinthians 10:12; Matthew 18:21-22;
Luke 18:11; 2 Corinthians 4:8-9; Isaiah
40:1; 55:8-9; Luke 13:4-5; Hebrews
12:11

*A*n established doctrine of the Old Testament which many people still tend to live by today is the fact that all human suffering presupposes corresponding sin. They say that all disaster is penalty for sins committed. The Hebrews believed that all things good and all things bad came from God—depending on whether he was pleased or displeased. Today we know that we should not judge the major sufferers to be the major sinners. Our major heroes are the martyrs who have made great sacrifices. It should be obvious that suffering is woven into the very fabric of life.

Through the centuries mankind has wrestled with the problem of God, man, suffering, and sin. Remember how Job's friends were so sure that he needed to confess his sins to God? They believed that God allowed trouble to fall exclusively on evil men. Job, however, was intellectually honest and questioned the old theory and thus a landmark was established in updating the theology of the Old Testament. This higher level rejected the idea that all personal suffering is personal punishment. Yes, sin brings its penalty in one form or another, but all personal suffering could not be traced back to personal sin. Both the Old Testament and New Testament agree that all wickedness brings trouble, but all trouble was not penalty for wickedness. In the end sinners suffered, but all those who suffered were not necessarily sinners.

The Psalms show a movement away from the old doctrine by a postponing of awards—a wait and you will see (Ps. 37). Isaiah lifted suffering from being primitive to being the source of redemption. In the Old Testament pain and sorrow started as disgrace and punishment and now Isaiah teaches that adversity and suffering can be redemptive. Isaiah himself was amazed at this revelation (Isa. 40:1; 55:8, 9).

Job was far ahead of his time in his theology. He didn't understand all that was going on, but he did believe in God and that was all he needed. Psalm 73 is also a beautiful testimony of human difficulty of dealing with adversity. The problem of evil is left as an intellectual mystery, but with the soul triumphant in the awareness of divine fellowship and hope.

The New Testament argues from sin to consequence, while the Old Testament argues from trouble back to a preceding sin as a necessary formula for explanation. Jesus denied this. He saw that some trouble falls on all without regard to morality (Luke 13:4, 5).

The fact that some trouble is disciplinary seems to be well accepted (Heb. 7:5-8). An untroubled life is an uneducated life. No painless life can be wise or strong or good; this theme runs throughout the New Testament. We should view troubles and pain as an implement for growth. Hebrews 12:11 states that discipline or trouble seems unpleasant at the time, but later produces a harvest of peace for those who have learned from it.

As Christians, we ought not to equate prosperity with goodness and adversity with badness, but rather positively use trouble for discipline and to strengthen the inner being. This way, trouble will not destroy you, but will polish and refine your life. With the kingdom of God in our hearts, we are assured of victory even in the face of disaster. We can agree with Paul (Rom. 8:38-39) that although we do not understand everything, we trust in God and nothing can separate us from his love.

Some people have sought out a religion that will allow them to escape trouble. However, we can see clearly by studying the teachings of Jesus that he calls his disciples to courses of action that involve suffering (Matt. 10:16; 5:11; 16:24). As we grow and experience all that life brings, we begin to understand that suffering is not in itself a curse but a vital element in living to the fullest. One major difference between man and lower animals is the capacity of man to suffer, to be sensitive. The aim of life should not be to abolish suffering, but to learn to make it useful, a stimulant in our creative processes to make us more like Jesus.

Many of us feel that as Christians we should never experience anxiety, temptation, crisis, trouble, anything that causes life to be less than smooth. We observe people who seem to have achieved a perfectly balanced life. They never seem to have any problems; their marriages are perfect, and so are their children.

Let's look closely at the term "perfectly balanced." Only if you're standing absolutely still are you balanced. Actually, only the dead are perfectly balanced. It would be monotonous to be always balanced. The people who seem to have perfect lives have insulated themselves by finding some sort of peace of mind. They don't understand the old spiritual "Sometimes I'm up, sometimes I'm down. O yes Lord."

Life, if you're really living, is like a pendulum, constantly swinging back and forth. The Christian has a fixed point from which life swings to and fro. It is the fixed point, Jesus Christ, that keeps us from totally going to pieces or flying off at one end or the other of the swing.

A lot of my time as a child was spent in a swing (and I still like it). It was attached securely by my father to a very high branch of a tree in our backyard. I learned to get myself started back and forth; I learned the fine art of "pumping"; I could stand up, pump and get going, and then sit down and keep going on and on, higher and higher. I pretended to see kingdoms, forests, animals, and all sorts of things on the upswings. I was helping my physical body grow and my imagination was stretched. It was fun and sometimes scary, especially while I learned the art of jumping out. But that swing never fell and I never worried about that. My father put it up and he would never want the swing that held me to be less than perfect for me. I only got hurt when I jumped out or fell out and landed wrong. On rainy days, I'd look out the window at my swing and relive the excitement of the wind rushing through my hair and think about the next time I'd be propelled up and then up some more. I was bored when I was not on the move.

Today I walked out in our backyard and sat down in the swing that was put up years ago for our sons by their father. It is still very secure and strong. Automatically my body began to move in the rhythmic "pumping" motions and I began to swing back and forth. You see, a swing is no fun to just sit in. It is made for movement.

Life is like that. It is made for movement. Our heavenly Father securely holds the "swing" while we learn to pump and take the jumps and falls.

To be a growing Christian we have to grow, take a step forward. Why else do we say "Walk with Christ" or label our discipleship as a "journey"? A dead person who is perfectly balanced does not grow and is soon buried. So we have a choice; take a walk, take a risk, open up and learn, or stand still, die, and be buried.

A Christian does, to be sure, have the peace, the joy of Christ in his heart and soul. But, he also often has a surging turmoil, real soul pain, and that doesn't mean he is weak. He will courageously put one foot in front of the other, always in tune to God's will, and get on through the difficulty. Lofton Hudson titles a chapter in one of his books, "The Courage of Imperfection."[1] I like that. Not only are we imperfect, but everything and everybody around us is imperfect. Our emotional and mental anguish comes when we think that we're living in a perfect world.

Growth is a slow process and frequently occurs in spurts.

This seems to be the process with physical and spiritual growth. Sometimes we try to hurry the process in ourselves or in others and that just seems to be a hindrance. If we learned from the chapter on self-esteem, we have made the initial step in growth. Learn to be "yourself," acknowledging that you can't be anyone else. Each flower is lovely, but a rose cannot be a daisy, etc. We must keep in mind the best picture of ourselves, revise it when needed, and grow toward that.

The next unit will deal specifically with growth in many areas. Times of stress or crisis can be seasons of growth spurts if we handle them sanely. All through life there will be upsetting, unsettling circumstances that will cause us to tense up, to grab for something to hold on to. We learn to look for alternatives. If the crisis is extremely traumatic we look for a tourniquet to stop the bleeding and then seek the road to healing.

An event becomes a crisis sometimes because of the way we interpret it. Job said it beautifully for most of us worriers: "What I feared has come upon me; what I dreaded has happened to me. I have no peace, no quietness; I have no rest, but only turmoil" (Job 3:25-26, NIV). Even Christians who are not bona fide, card-carrying worriers learn through ordinary daily living to take a hard look at reality in order not to be totally caught off guard. We learn to "sandbag" for the waves of stress that just normally come.

After the initial shock/surprise of a crisis situation, alternatives must be sought. Sometimes several have to be tried and then when we've stabilized the situation enough to think more clearly a big decision may have to be made. Through all of this process we must be open to God. He is walking with us through all life situations.

Crisis situations are so frightening because they threaten our selfhood. We ask ourselves questions such as "What did I do wrong?"; "What will people think of me/us?"; "What will I do?"; "Who can help me?"; "I'd rather be dead than go through this." Eventually, our faith will come thundering through and we'll begin to search for alternatives; we'll begin to get our act together and plow on through with God's help.

This means that we have to take some risks. Usually, a crisis or stress situation does not allow one to be over cautious. This is why it is important to always have the communication of prayer with the Father. This is the time for "gut" feeling decisions. If you discover that your decision was definitely wrong, then be open to changing your mind. Don't pretend that you're always right—even to your spouse and children. Allow God to act creatively through you even in times of stress and pain.

Faith in God is deepened and strengthened when we are stretched and forced to grapple with crises. The way we handle crises may make us or break us; we will learn and grow or shrink and die. Faith will help us get the proper perspective in any situation.

After you have faced the crisis situation there may be a time of lengthy waiting. We make adjustments in life to handle this. It is truly amazing how much the person with deep faith can endure if he becomes flexible and cooperative with God.

What can we do to help ourselves and others in crisis situations? Here are some suggestions from both experience and observation.

1.  Don't try to come up with a quick, easy answer. You can't give any answer to the automatic question that literally gushes out of the one in pain "Why? Why? Why me? Why my child/parent/spouse?" You really don't know why, so don't try to play God and answer anyway. For goodness sake, don't use those tacky catch-all phrases such as, "Don't cry, it's God's will"; "It could be a lot worse"; "I know just how you feel."

2.  You can say, "I don't understand this, either, but I'm going to walk through it with you. I'm here if you need me." You can give your love and support, but no sugar-coated phrases, please. Allow the person (or yourself) to be

angry at the situation, or at the person, or at God. Yes, that's right, angry with God. God understands that and he is just waiting to comfort and lead through the path of learning.

3. Learn to listen and never repeat what you hear. Don't feel obligated to console or advise; just be there to listen and to be a leaning post. Be an uncritical listener. I have had people tell me what I should have done or where I went wrong. I can live without those people and those comments. I did the best I knew to do at the time. That's all anyone can do.

4. It is important that you be authentic and sincere and spontaneous when helping someone in trouble. Even an hysterical person can sense phoniness. Trust the leadership of the Holy Spirit in aiding you to be an effective helper and friend. The typical counseling phrases (How did that make you feel?) are no good. Be with the person and allow him to bleed and whimper in your presence.

5. If you are trustworthy and authentic, the person will want you to help him look at all his alternatives. You can be a big help and perhaps offer some that he was not aware of. Be sure you allow him to make the decisions; he has to tolerate the circumstances, not you.

6. Know some good sources of help. It may be church resources, community, physicians, attorneys, whatever. Learn where to go for help, both short-term and long-term.

We've talked mostly about how to help others in crisis times. What can we do for ourselves? Well, one thing to remember is that if you live and breathe you will have to face these times. So, the best thing you can do for yourself is to learn some very practical coping devices. Develop your resources for coping. I think the number one thing to do is to develop an ongoing, close relationship with the heavenly Father. Learn to trust him with your life. This may sound morbid, but it needs to be said. One of these days you'll find yourself in such a crisis that you'll wonder if you will survive. You may not. The illness, accident, etc., may be terminal. We never know which crisis situation will be the one that we do not live through. If you have a close relationship with the Father, you won't have to be afraid to die. It will be like going home.

Remember that God has a providence and we must learn to cope and sort of flow with the circumstances. It is important for children, adolescents, and young adults to develop their coping devices. Too often, parents take all the burden of problems and troubles and don't allow the young to learn to cope. These lessons must be learned from an early age—just like walking alone, feeding oneself, etc. Learn early to trust the flow of life. Do all things possible to make it right and then relax in God's care.

Not only do you need to learn to trust God, but you also need to learn to trust yourself. Have confidence in yourself that you will be able to cope with whatever life brings. Yes, you may have trouble with it, but you know deep down that you won't be overwhelmed, that you will ultimately handle it with God's help. You need to know that you *can* face tomorrow.

Crisis situations abound. There seem to be new ones invented every day. Crises range from making a failing grade at school to having to have your leg amputated; from having your house robbed to discovering that your best friend has betrayed you; from being confronted by an angry neighborhood mother because of the children's quarrels to being confronted at your front door by the police who say your daughter was picked up hitchhiking. Troubles come with the ringing of the telephone. "Your mother is dying"; "Your son is in jail"; "Dear, I'll be working late tonight, don't wait dinner"; "Your husband was in Houston with someone he introduced as his wife"; "Your wife has been in an accident." Crises come in the forms of cancer, financial problems, domestic situations, illness of children, rebellious adolescents, alcoholism, drug addiction, mental illness, old age, accidents, divorce, imprisonment, sexual deviations, death, and life, to mention only a few.

The big problem is that when we're submerged in one of these crisis situations we feel like we're all alone, no one has ever experienced this before, no one can possibly understand, and certainly God doesn't even care. If we can come up for air for a minute and reach up for help, both from human friends and God, we'll be on the road to making it. Always have hope. Without hope, you can't survive.

[1] Lofton Hudson, *Helping Each Other Be Human* (Waco: Word Books, 1969).

## Work Space

1. Read 2 Corinthians 4:8-9
   What does this say about crises and our lives?


   Do you think that Paul understood about trouble?


   Can you identify with this Scripture?

2. After reading the section on being helpful to those in crisis situations, how would you handle these? If you are in a group, act out the parts. Feel free to change to a situation you know about first-hand.
   a. The couple is young and they have one child who has been injured in a hit-and-run accident. The child is in critical condition.
   b. Husband and wife are facing the very real possibility of having to put her mother in a nursing home. The mother needs round-the-clock nursing care. It is a traumatic time, filled with feelings of guilt, grief, failure, etc.
   c. Husband faces wife of thirty-two years with request for divorce in order to marry his mistress of seven years (unknown to wife). Wife goes to pieces; three grown children are caught in middle; help is needed.
   d. Young couple, no children, very volatile and head-strong. Always fighting over everything, anything. She packs up and goes home to Mother, but isn't happy about it. Is there help for them? Any hope?

3. This week pray for your spouse, your marriage, and related needs. Pray for the couple now seated on your left by name this week.

# 11. The Honeymoon Is Over–The Early Years

*Bible Passages:*  Proverbs 1:8; Deuteronomy 6:6-7; 2 Chronicles 26:3-4; 1 Corinthians 7:3-4; Mark 7:9-13; Matthew 19:1; 1 Timothy 5:8; 2 Timothy 1:5; Ephesians 6:1-4; 4:31-32

*I*n 1979 one out of three married couples between the ages of twenty-five and thirty-five were divorced. It is estimated that two out of five children born in the late seventies will spend at least five years with a single parent.

The increasing mobility of our culture has cut into the basic securities of life—family and long-term friendships. We develop calluses over our heart hungers so that we can function in this upheaval without having to expose our basic fears and frustrations. We need the family unit now more than ever to survive our culture. Marriage provides a unit for community, for psychological and emotional survival and support. Combining romantic love with the challenge of survival is an awesome task. The romantic idea portrayed in advertising gives the impression that the couple is always young (and beautiful, of course), carefree, happy, no worries, no responsibilities, and an unending desire and capacity for making love. "And they lived happily ever after" is a myth that we try to believe in. Actually, if a couple truly works at it, gives the marriage time and space, it really could be true in retrospect.

Do you remember the poet Dante, who fell in love with Beatrice at nine years old? The sight of her unearthly beauty (to him) remained with him forever and she became his heroine, his angel of his writings, even though he did marry someone else. What would have happened if he had married Beatrice and she had been a human wife to him in good and bad times, instead of the angel of his creative imagination? That's the way we are in our marriage relationships. We dream and imagine one thing—the perfect. Reality is a different story. The early years of marriage bring us sharply to face reality and sometimes the reality is so disappointing and we're so disenchanted and disillusioned that we succumb to the temptation to run away.

Many people anticipate more in marriage than is possible to deliver. More than one person has walked down the aisle to meet one person at the altar and walked out with that one having become a total stranger. What a person expects in marriage is usually a fulfillment of one's heart hungers whether one is aware of this or not—for instance, financial fears, parental substitute, or loneliness.

The average marriage begins to settle down and lose its euphoric glow rather quickly. Some couples have great disillusionment from the very beginning, even as they leave the church. To some the honeymoon represents the very peak of the marriage relationship and it's all downhill from there. The loss of novelty and excitement seems to encompass almost every aspect of the relationship, with sex at the top of the list. Some marriages deteriorate from this point, and others with more mature partners involved begin the journey of growth and nourishment for each other.

The average newly married couple first experience a short blissful period where the emphasis is a *mutual enjoyment.* Next they move into a *mutual adjustment* period and hopefully work out differences and conflicts. If this adjustment period is successful, then they can move on to a new stage of *mutual fulfillment,* using the insights and understanding of each other they have gained from their experiences together.

How a couple deals with early difficulties greatly affects their marriage in the middle years.

The honeymoon is an extension of the courtship. Good

manners and diplomacy are still intact and used. Little by little, however, we let romantic images slip and becoming more and more comfortable, we forget to be gracious and become argumentative. One couple put it this way: *"One thing we had to learn early was that being comfortable with each other does not mean we can be slovenly."* Example: husband slopping around with uncombed hair and torn T-shirt; wife plastering her face with cream and sleeping with hair in rollers.

The things that could be tolerated once in a while now become all the time and it is no longer cute, but a screaming annoyance. Those little peculiar habits or the opposite qualities that attracted us at the beginning now get on our nerves. Then, if we try to be open and honest and really communicate, that is fine until "he starts criticizing my mother." Or, "why can't you shut the dresser drawer when you're finished digging?" Finding the toilet seat up (or down) or leaving the tub handle on "shower" instead of "tub" and getting a wet head is very trying on the nerves. All those trivial but very common everyday things, which now have to be given a second thought, become grounds for thunderous fights if not worked out in a sane and agreeable way.

There is a system of interaction that each couple evolves with the growth of the marriage. The couple is never really aware that it is happening or that it is visible to observers. It involves things like who defers to whom, what is allowable in conversation and behavior, how each pricks the other's sore points, etc. You can observe this in others, but one can hardly recognize one's own system.

Some couples cling to the mirage that everything is perfect in the marriage, rather than make the effort to develop the relationship that allows one to be "stark naked" to at least one person emotionally in the security that he will still accept and care for me with all my faults. One doesn't have to pretend any more. This frees one to realize greater potential because one doesn't have to feel guilty or stupid. This leads to one of the needs of couples in the early years of marriage.

*It is important to establish each one's need for space.* Husband and wife have to work out the balance of "how much space I need" and "how much space is appropriate" so that both will be comfortable with it. The balance may change or shift in various degrees through the years. The idea of allowing room to grow within the relationship (never to the detriment of the relationship) must be dealt with early in the marriage. Otherwise one will outgrow the other, overwhelm the other, as will be discussed in the lesson on the "middle years."

In close connection with the idea of allowing each other appropriate space is also the problem of the couple establishing joint identity while keeping self-identity. Any close relationship, but especially marriage, can be choked to death by being held too tightly. We mentioned togetherness earlier, but husband, wife, and children cannot all think exactly alike on everything. It would be like the "Bobbsey Twins" reproduced over and over. One of our sons was asked by a well-meaning adult friend, "What do you want to be when you grow up?" and the six-year-old answered without batting an eye, "Me." It is important to be "me" and then to be "us." Each couple must constantly be alert to each other and allow the "me" and the "us" to evolve as the relationship matures.

Too often a couple in the early years of marriage assume that the honeymoon was the height of their sexual enjoyment. If that were the truth, many couples would be extremely disappointed and heartsick. You have to get used to each other sexually; you have to discover what pleases and never be embarrassed or ashamed to tactfully teach each other. If this is begun in the early years, many of the problems, the disappointments, and sadness of the middle and later years will never occur. If there are problems in this area (or any other) seek help now, don't wait for a crisis. The grinding pressures that just normally come with living take their toll on marriage and especially on sexual intimacy. This is, of course, the most intimate communication of husband and wife and the giving and receiving pleasure and love nourishes every area of the relationship. You will have to learn to create occasions for loving because time and fatigue will rob you of a precious gift.

Something else that has to be hammered out in this early period is how to settle differences. Go back and read the lesson on "How to Fuss and Fight Fairly." There are some couples (one or the other, or both) who come from a super pious background and try to build a home on religious principles who are totally frustrated because they do have to face some unpleasant, disagreeable things. Rather than work them out, they pretend they aren't there and try to maintain a show of peace and calm to themselves and the world. Any close relationship demands a working out of conflicts. Exaggerated need for harmony at home is not what the New Testament teaches. It teaches that life is filled with alienation, reconciliation, and forgiveness. That is where we need to put our emphasis and learn early in marriage how this works.

In a survey I recently conducted in relation to these lessons, I found the overwhelming cause for disagreement among young marrieds to be money. It seems that it is not necessarily how much money as it is what is yours, mine, and ours. How the money is handled, how the bills are paid, how much to save, etc., are fragmenting to a marriage. Settle, or at least learn to communicate about finances now during the early years so that the conflicts over money won't persist long after the time when budgets are not so necessary or strictly enforced. As the years go by, needs change, income usually increases, and extreme tension over finances should ease, but if there is no communication other than conflict, the problem will get worse with time.

Another cause for serious conflict among young marrieds is the need for *being weaned from parents*. If this is not accomplished early, the resulting hard feelings between husband and wife can become almost irreconcilable. One of the saddest comments I received in the survey among young marrieds was this: "Fuss and fight about most? In-laws. When should wife be put first in husband's affections; when should mother be put first?" The old saying, "there is no cleaving without leaving" is absolutely true. A parent who holds a grown child like a puppet by the strings is emotionally immature and the grown child who is blind to this is emotionally sick.

A young couple also has to *learn to accept comments (advice) from parents and family without feeling threatened or feeling like you have to act on it.* Learn to receive the comment, information, whatever, and file it in your mind to use or let it in one ear and out the other. When you're a married adult, you have to be mature enough to allow you and your spouse to make your own decisions and if you make mistakes, you'll be mature enough to handle them. Your parents have had the privilege of living their own lives, now you must live yours. This is true in money areas, house buying, furniture purchases, child rearing, vacations, etc.

During the early years of marriage the couple has to set many priorities. These include determining the *ratio or mix of work, recreation, church, time alone, time with spouse, and time with children.* This is constantly in flux, but it has to be dealt with realistically. Careers can eat up all your time if one is not aware of it or if this is the top priority. Large corporations are notoriously bad about demanding first claim on their employees no matter how far up the ladder they are.

Sometimes in these first years (the first ten anyway) the birth of a child causes great excitement, happiness, and trauma. Needless to say, this will affect every area of life. Nothing will ever be the same again. Now there are several things that need to be faced very honestly. There are women to whom motherhood is all they ever desired out of life and they enjoy everything about being pregnant and delivering and nursing and changing diapers. Those of us who are a little different feel "put down" and less than we should be if we acknowledge that it isn't all that wonderful to us. I realize I risk all sorts of criticism, but I do think that the women who are not totally happy with being pregnant and all that it entails need some assurance that they aren't the only ones in the world who feel that way. It does not mean that you are any less of a woman or that you love your children any less. It's just one of those personality differences. Whether you're ecstatically happy or working on it, the real fact is that both wife and husband are in for some real changes. The routine will be interrupted and reorganized numerous times. There are many books and articles to aid the new mother and father in learning to cope with that new advent.

If you're a parent, you need special help. There are general, flexible guidelines that would be helpful in child rearing. Parenting should be taught by parents, using sound guidelines with ample flexibility to allow for wide variances in families. Those teaching should be trained to teach the group and this is best done in the curriculum of the Sunday School or Church Training—certainly under the auspices of your church. If you need help and desire consultations with counselors or need references to good books, please call your church for help.

I asked a group of young adults in our church to write a letter to a friend who is expecting their first baby, giving some ideas about how it really is and some suggestions. Here are some excerpts from their letters:

**#1**

"The biggest surprise of my experience in becoming a mother was that nothing was the way I had imagined it to be. Seven years later, this fact is still true. This was the vision: I would glow with radiant health while pregnant. I would enjoy a mind-expanding experience during the delivery of my baby and would love the pampering my doting husband would lavish on me afterward. I would take perfect care of this new life, relishing every minute of every day, and naturally, she would bring nothing but joy to an already happy marriage. She would wear pink gingham and lace and as she grew older would follow me around the house saying, 'I love you, Mommy.' She would be very good for my ego.

"This is the reality: I threw up—a lot! I forgot what it

was like to feel good. Our sex life was temporarily slipped to one side. I was asleep during delivery, took my baby home the following day and moved from Florida to Tennessee when she was six days old. My husband (who has never before or since been doting) did not pamper us. We couldn't afford pink gingham and lace, and when the baby grew older, she followed me around the house saying, 'What can I do now?' Our blessing from heaven brought us great joy, but the 'nothing but' portion of the phrase was asking too much. She also brought a loss of privacy, and a feeling of confinement, and a lot of hard work.

"Here is the good part. It *was* different than I expected it to be. It was harder. The joy that I anticipated, however, is even more intense than I dreamed possible. This baby, and the one that followed, have been our motivation to keep our priorities in order. We knew they would bless and enrich our lives; we did not know to what extent. Praise be to God!"

**#2**

"Having your first child is a great thrill, but it is also a very sobering experience. Your first thoughts are of how much you want to have a child, but then the reality of the awesome responsibility hits you and that's frightening.

"Some of the feelings are: Can I provide for my family? Will my child be healthy? What can I do to help my wife during this time? How will this child change our lifestyle? Can I truly adjust my lifestyle? How will I be with a baby to care for? I don't know anything about caring for a baby. Can I live with my wife during this time?

"These are all very honest and normal feelings. The only really good advice that I can give is that you will survive all of these and many more, but the most important thing to remember is that your wife is the most important person during this time."

**#3**

"As a new mother, I felt like I was often neglecting my husband. The attention I would have given to him now was centered on the new baby. It was as if I could 'love' just so much and there wasn't enough to be divided! This feeling didn't last very long, but it really bothered me. However, in talking to my husband about it later, he said he never felt neglected, so the feeling was one I alone experienced.

"Of course, the sheer physical responsibility of being a mother is overwhelming! It takes most babies a few weeks to even think about sleeping through the night. I think I got used to less sleep! Then the wonderful morning comes when you realize you have slept all night!

"There was a big change socially. You can't go out so easily any more. Things have to be a bit more planned—not so 'spur-of-the-moment.' We took our baby many places with us, but also used a babysitter at times. This is very important! The two of you need time together without the baby. It really helps in making for good relationships for everyone involved.

"We had to adjust our lifestyle financially. With both of us working, we ate out frequently because we both enjoyed it and it was more convenient at times. Without my salary, we're limited to eating out much less.

"Getting places on time became a problem. A good rule is to figure out how long you think it will take you to get ready, then add at least thirty minutes! I have tried to get everything ready the night before, which really helps. On Saturday night I get diaper bags packed, clothes laid out, etc., so that the next morning I don't have to try to remember everything!

"One change I was worried about was that I was afraid I'd really miss my job. I had thoroughly enjoyed teaching and have had a few moments when I missed my classroom. But, I have found being a parent to be one of the most rewarding things I could ever do. I wouldn't miss the joy of being at home with my children for anything! They change so quickly, and every stage of their lives is different. I will probably return to teaching when my children are older, but for now I'm happy at home. Of course, always being at home would be tiring. I have several 'outlets,' mostly at church, where I can teach and work with other people and this is very important.

"We have found that being parents has brought much joy to our lives and has brought us closer together as a couple. We have shared the responsibility of trying to provide a warm, loving, Christian home where our children are guided to become their best selves."

### #4

"While your wife is pregnant, she needs to feel pretty. Notice the little things such as her hair, her dress, how neat the house is. All those little details make her feel better when she is getting so big and feels like a blubber tub.

"Your child needs your time. You must not put off the opportunities to play with your children and to start teaching them. Your children will grow up before you know it. Never put off the chance to teach them or play with them. Remember that your conduct is what your child perceives to be right for a father and a husband. Your love, your attention, and your prayers are necessary to be a successful father."

### #5

"I'm sure you've heard the expression, 'It's the age or the stage.' Babies—and all children—will go through stages of not eating well, getting into everything, being sassy, and not wanting to mind. Rather than ignoring it as a 'stage,' I really feel it's up to the parents to adjust and set guidelines as to how to handle the child at that time so that all will be better able to cope with the situation. All the while we need to remember when these changes occur. The child is growing, maturing, and usually it's the parents who also need to 'grow' along with the child at each age and interest level.

"I have always felt that children were a special gift from God. I guess if a baby is unplanned, it's hard to accept that idea. Maybe you really don't want the gift! Yet I feel God has some special plan in mind for you, as there are many who want children that God didn't choose to bless with a child. It's very important to put things in the proper perspective—God as the head of your home, set a good example for your children, have prayer and Bible reading in the home, take the children to church at an early age, and seek God's guidance that he will lead you in child rearing as in all other phases of life. Sing choruses, read Bible stories from an early age so that the child will grow up with these implanted in his mind!

"Another area which may be of major concern is finances, especially if you had planned to work longer than you're going to be able to and had counted on that second income. I think from the beginning of marriage it would do couples well to think in terms of their income just being that of the husband and live in keeping with that one paycheck, simply for reasons like this. Even if you plan to go back to work, in case of a child illness, etc., it's usually the mother who stays home. If you are able to work, think of your salary as being 'extra,' but I think it's easier if you don't become so dependent on it from the beginning. The best brand name, the latest model, etc., isn't a necessity and your lives can be just as happy and fulfilling without material things. Believe me, I know. A lot of people ask us how we make it on one salary and when I reply by saying that we first take out one-tenth for the church and operate on the rest, they are amazed. We've always been able to manage. God cares for his own."

After the birth of our first child I was not well. My hair was falling out, my skin was dry, and I had all kinds of problems. But the most frightening thing of all was that I couldn't remember anything. If I drove myself to the doctor, I would forget where I parked the car. I was afraid that I would forget to turn the stove off and burn the house down or hurt the baby in some way because of my forgetting. Finally, after running the gamut of being told that a minister's wife shouldn't have problems, so I must be a bad person (that actually happened), to all sorts of tests, we found out I had a problem thyroid. A tiny yellow pill taken daily restored my sanity—and my memory and hair!

Many times there are medical reasons for problems people have that make them react strangely. There are also emotional problems that result in great trauma for the family. One of the most horrifying problems that we see more of today (it is not a new phenomenon) is child abuse. You are probably thinking, "Why do we need this, we're all Christians?" That may be true, but that doesn't mean that you are free from all emotional or chemical dysfunction.

Parents who abuse their children have one common characteristic. They were themselves battered children, either physically or emotionally. They could never please their parents however much they tried, but they acquired the conviction that children exist to please parents and when they don't, they are beaten either physically or with words. So these battered children grow up to be child abusers. Children (they were taught) are to please me. When he cries, wets his diaper, etc., it's a personal offense. Not only does the child need help, but the parent needs to feel loved and accepted to overcome the rejection he experienced.

If you are ever frightened by the way you feel about your children—if you feel like you're going to explode and you're afraid of what you may do, please call a friend you can trust, your pastor or Sunday School teacher, someone who can get you the help you need. Sometimes it is just that you are physically exhausted. Perhaps you need a sitter so you can get away from the house and children for a while. Don't feel guilty. The only reason to feel guilty is if you don't do something to change the situation.

During these early years, a couple may look forward to planning a family only to discover that for some reason the wife is not able to conceive. This is disappointing and some hard words may be said, feelings may be hurt, and one or both may feel guilty. Be sure you have the best help available and that the husband is included in the testing. Whatever route you may decide to follow under the guidance of your physician (specialist in this area), remember that this desire to have a child must not become an all-consuming obsession. If your satisfaction and happiness depends on whether or not you become parents, you'd better reexamine your relationship.

Some couples today are choosing not to have children. They may do this for a number of good reasons. This is a very personal decision and no one should criticize or ask cruel questions. The main thing is that both husband and wife agree on this so that one will not feel cheated and angry about it.

Some couples choose not to have children because they marry late and both have fulfilling careers. Another may have a family history of physical or emotional problems that they do not wish to risk on a child. Some may feel an overwhelming sense of fear and inadequacy and fear losing control of themselves. Some people just do not feel that they should bring another human being into this high risk world. These are only a few reasons people give for remaining childless. A couple should not have a child only to satisfy the grandparenting need for their parents or just because "we're expected to have a child at this stage in life."

There are many alternatives to being "natural" parents. Nieces and nephews need your attention. Children of your divorced or widowed friends need extra love. Teaching children in Sunday School, scouting, church activities, sports, and many other areas offer opportunities to reach out and love children. Often a child will open up to an adult rather than a parent and you can be an important part of his life. Also, you would be greatly loved and appreciated if you would take care of the children of friends or family occasionally so their parents can get away and truly relax, knowing their children are loved and cared for.

One of the results of the survey on what do couples fuss and fight about showed that many have trouble over *child rearing* (care and treatment of the child) and *responsibilities for the running of the household* (when both work). Since most of us cannot afford housekeepers (and where would we find one?), this is a problem that won't go away and it must be resolved responsibly. Some things about housekeeping can be put off, but too often husband or wife will procrastinate and the other feels "put upon."

A change is taking place in family roles in many homes. As more wives work, either because of career goals or because of financial needs, more husbands are going to work at home. They are sharing household chores, management, and also nurturing tasks that have traditionally fallen to women alone. Today many men are involved in the whole range of household duties including cooking, cleaning, shopping, and caring for children. Not all men enjoy these jobs, nor do all men do them, but many younger men (more than older men who have been married a long time) take pride in their accomplishments and believe that sharing chores has helped their marriage.

Many men readily acknowledge that they would be content to sit back and bask in the glories that have traditionally been bestowed on the breadwinner, if it weren't for the fact that their wives are out there earning bread, too. The women's movement has nothing to do with the physical and emotional stamina needed to keep home running smoothly. It is impossible for a woman not to feel angry if she has to come home after working all day and do all the housework and cooking while her husband watches television. Her anger will soon show up in their relationship.

*The Wall Street Journal* recently had an article concerning this. They had interviewed a number of couples and some of the ways of handling chores were interesting. The article pointed out that men who marry late are more likely to want to share responsibility of the housekeeping chores. One couple (he is thirty-three and a bank vice president; she is thirty-five and a museum curator) live in a three-bedroom house and naturally gravitated toward the tasks each preferred. She is the house cleaner and handyman and he is in charge of food. They have no children.

She found it hard to cut the apron strings and leave him to the kitchen, but she has adjusted and occasionally catches herself falling into the "male thing" of sulking if dinner isn't on the table when she gets home! Since he does the cooking, he naturally does the shopping. They are very happy with this arrangement with each doing what they are best suited to do.

One couple with a baby eighteen months told about their partnership. Each morning Jane dresses the baby while her husband, Dick, showers; Dick feeds the baby while Jane showers. Jane packs the baby's lunch and Dick takes him to the sitter. In the evening Jane picks up the baby and starts dinner while Dick plays with the baby; then after dinner, Dick cleans up the dishes while Jane plays with the baby. They both take the baby for walks after the dishes are done. This couple are both managers of businesses and this is carried over into their home.

In all but the most nontraditional homes there seems to be the underlying assumption that in spite of all the sharing, the woman holds the ultimate responsibility for the home. For example: a huge rainstorm came up and the wife dashed home to make sure the basement wasn't flooded. It never occurred to her husband.

Many husbands are made fun of and suffer humiliating remarks if their housework sharing is known. Executives do not like it to be known that they share parenting responsibilities because corporations have not faced this trend.

When both husband and wife work, whether because of dual career goals or for purely financial need, they must face these questions squarely and realistically deal with them. There is only so much physical and emotional energy and everyone will get shortchanged if this is not handled properly.

## Work Space

1.  (Group) What did you expect marriage to be like?

2.  (Personal) What is it like?

3.  If you have been married before: Is this marriage different? How?

4.  Write two things that could be better in your marriage. Discuss with spouse. Is she/he surprised? How can these be helped?

5.  Groups divide into groups—couples separated. Discuss assigned case studies.

6.  Do you both have a career or both work outside the home? If so, are you able to divide the household chores satisfactorily? How can it be better?

7.  Are you both doing well at cutting the parental cord? Are you becoming weaned from your parents? Discuss this honestly with each other.

8.  If you have a child: Are you making sure that your spouse receives some of your attention? Do you feel neglected? How? Talk about this.

9.  If you have no children: Are you enjoying each other, and are you aware that you can be helpful to children of family and friends?

**Case Studies**

Can you see the danger points? Can you relate to any of them? How can they be helped?

1.  The phone rang late on a Monday evening when my husband was out of town overnight for a Foreign Mission Board meeting. A young man asked to speak to the pastor. When he heard that Bill was not available, he sounded so panic-stricken that I asked if he needed one of the other ministers. He blurted out that his wife (they have been married about a year) had just told him she wanted a divorce and that she planned to see a lawyer the next day. He wanted them to talk to the pastor first. He acknowledged that they had been having trouble. His business had failed and he had been out of work, but he had a job now and had no idea she would ask for a divorce. Neither had sought help earlier. Now, he was desperately grasping for help and hope.

    Money is often the problem that brings out trouble in other areas. If one spouse senses that the other is irresponsible in the financial area, the fear of poverty, or of having to face family and friends with "my husband is out of work"; "we can't afford a house (or vacation, or children, or whatever)" is too humiliating. It seems easier to get out before being overwhelmed by debts. Money also means power. If you can't manage to get and keep and use it properly, you lose the right to power.

2.  They had planned and prayed for the baby. Up to this point everything had been smooth sailing. They both had good jobs, had saved for a house, had just moved in (hadn't even had time to meet the neighbors) and then it all caved in. The baby was stillborn. They were crushed. They consoled each other and the doctor was optimistic about her being able to have a healthy baby later. The husband learned an even deeper love for her because he had feared for her life also. Family and friends and church

family supported them. Now eighteen months later they are the happy, thankful parents of a fine, healthy son. Illness, death, and disappointment can create such problems with one or both that a great rift occurs in the marriage. It all depends on how you cope.

3. Jane was crushed. They had only been married a couple of months and Dan called to say he wouldn't be home after lunch on Saturday. He was going to play golf with the guys. "I'll be by to get my clubs in a few minutes." Needless to say, she greeted him in tears, "How can you go play golf with them? I thought we'd spend the afternoon together. How could you leave me alone?" So he leaves, feeling awful, but the friends are waiting in the car. Both husband and wife have a miserable afternoon and the evening promises to be a disaster. Help! Their expectations of the relationship are different. Their past experiences based on observing their own families do not coincide. They need to plan together.

4. "Pastor, I just don't love him any more. If it wasn't for hurting him, I would leave him. I know he loves me, but I don't know what to do. I thought I loved him when I married him. I don't dislike him, I just don't feel anything for him. He says he will do anything to win me back. I feel awful spending three years with a man and then telling him I don't love him. I really hate to hurt him."

A counselor has to discover several things. Is she involved with someone else? If not, when, how, and why did the communication gap occur; or, can they learn to communicate? What is the real underlying problem—why can't she feel love for him, or, can she feel love for anyone? This statement, "I just don't love him anymore," is heard frequently by those who counsel. This marriage needs to grow through communication. They need to discover the real reasons behind her lack of ability to feel and for his apathy. She may be screaming, "Show me you care, that you really want me."

5. Lisa, a young wife and mother, was under terrific emotional strain when her husband of eight years brought her to the hospital. As her therapist, I heard her finally become able to verbalize her guilt and fears. I had observed that she reverted to childlike behavior in relating to the other patients. The only role she was secure in was that of a child, and here she was a wife and mother! Her husband, under the guise of love and concern, demanded that she account for every minute of her day to him: where she went, who she saw, what they said, and on and on. Yet she was responsible for their children and he expected maturity in that area. A crisis was bound to occur. Perhaps with counseling (to which he grudgingly is coming) they will learn to communicate with each other and relate to each other as adults. Whether or not she can tolerate the home situation remains to be seen.

6. Tom arrived on our doorstep desperately seeking a tourniquet for his bleeding ego. His company had transferred him to Atlanta and this was the transfer he had to take or leave the company. Tom and his wife, Dotti, had been married six years. Both were making great strides in their careers. Dotti felt that her career was important to her right now and that she could not risk losing her position and having to work her way up again in Atlanta. They had discussed their career goals and priorities before marriage, but never really believed they would have to face this crisis. Now Tom and Dotti are in a holding pattern. They alternate weekends between Atlanta and Houston, but the separation and travel is beginning to wear them down. Now, when they are together their tempers flare quickly and their relationship is becoming intolerable, but they love each other. This will be a diffi-

cult face-saving situation. They must both learn to compromise and decide what is really important to them—together and separately.

7. Ellen and Duke were married five years before their first baby, a daughter, was born. She was a difficult baby. She didn't sleep well and cried a lot; and the shock to the rather placid life-style of the prebaby stage was over-whelming. No one got much sleep and the demands of the baby were a nerve-shattering experience. Then, to their disbelief, Ellen was pregnant again. How could they endure another baby within seventeen months? Would Ellen survive emotionally and physically? Would Duke be so sick of all work, no play, constant turmoil, little sleep, lots of diapers and bottles that he would make working late at the office a habit and haven?

   This is one of life's stages, and it will pass. The serious problem is not to let the marriage pass. She will feel guilty and try to cover over her feelings of frustration and anger and of "not being a good mother." He will feel guilty and helpless and resentful. They must make time to be alone, to communicate, and drop their parental role temporarily.

8. Jan and Henry have been married about three years. Both have good jobs. He is an engineer and she worked to help him through the last year of his five-year engineering course. He has been out of school for two years now and she wants to start a family. He wants more time—several years—without family responsibilities. She accuses him of being more interested in money than in her happiness and needs. He, in turn, accuses her of not understanding about money and of being irresponsible. From there the arguing goes on to deal with nagging about household chores (he's not holding up his end in light of the full-time job) and sexual problems (she is unresponsive to his advances; he feels rejected; she wishes he were more

tender and interested in her as a person). They are both hurting and desperately desire more closeness, yet they retreat into frustrated isolation. Jan and Henry are bright and both desire a lot from their relationship. With help, they will be able to work through their frustration and differences and reach out and really touch each other. They will then be better prepared for becoming parents.

9.  Amy and Bill returned from their honeymoon in the heart of battle. Amy was twenty-eight and had a promising music career. Bill was thirty-six, had always lived with his mother, and was a highly successful stockbroker. It was the first marriage for both. Amy could not believe her competition—his mother! Bill had called her every day while they were away—an overseas call! He also was a perfectionist about everything. "Don't put anything down for even a moment because he will swoop it up and put it where it belongs, or in the trash," she reported. She was ready to pack and leave him to his mother. He really loved her, though, and didn't want to lose her. They have worked for years with a counselor, putting family (parents) and work and idiosyncrasies in their proper places. They have really worked at making their marriage fulfilling, and now (at least ten years later) they are able to joke about their shaky beginnings. Communication is the key. They are both very verbal and had no problem expressing themselves once they found the proper direction.

10. Tony and Leah are a handsome couple from good families who really care about their children. This is the problem. Whenever Tony or Leah are around their parents they become children again. Tony's dad is happy to be a confidant and freely offers advice, which he expects to be followed. In fact, Tony is more likely to tell his dad about his marital problems than he is to even mention them to Leah. Dad thinks Leah gives Tony a hard time and demands too much help from him around the

house. Leah is very close to her mother and confides that she just can't understand why Tony reacts the way he does when she asks him to help her or to go somewhere with her. Leah doesn't understand why Tony doesn't like the dress her mother bought for her or the new shoes her mother chose for her. Tony and Leah, both from good backgrounds, have a lot to build on once they are able to break away from their parents. It would probably be good for their marriage if they lived in another state for several years. They must each become independent adults, not ignoring their families, but functioning securely in a separate manner. They need to begin their own family traditions and styles, not necessarily like either family. Trying to unite two vastly different family styles can be very frustrating. Tony and Leah must learn to depend on each other for moral support first and also to keep certain elements of their life inside their own walls. Some things are not discussed with others, not even well-meaning parents or other family.

11. Sarah is overwhelmed. She has married into a wealthy family of demonstrative, vocal people. Her husband, Jeff, works for his father and so his parents feel they have a right to participate actively in the marriage of Sarah and Jeff. When they returned from their honeymoon, their apartment had been completely furnished, even down to the linen on the bed and towels in the bath, by Jeff's mother. His mother could not understand why Sarah was not totally thrilled over this. Now his mother is looking for a house for the family to buy for them. The ultra closeness of the family is making Sarah react to everything hysterically. Jeff feels caught in the middle—between his wife and his mother. He will be forced to make a choice unless one or the other or both back off or unless Sarah makes good her threat to leave. Sarah's question is, "When should a husband side with his wife instead of his mother?" She shouldn't even have to ask the question.

# 12. The Middle Years

*Bible Passages:* Psalm 25:4-5; 142:1-2, 6-7; 138-6-8

*U*ntil recent years, it was pretty well accepted that if a couple could stay together for the first five to eight years, they would make it together for the rest of their lives. Now, hardly a week goes by without some of us in our communities hearing the unbelievable news that a couple married eighteen, twenty, even thirty-five years is breaking up. Everyone begins to speculate about what went wrong, who had been unfaithful to whom (this is a given assumption), how will the husband and wife manage, and on and on. Underneath the spoken questions, however, is the painful inward query, "Could this (will this) happen to me?" This fear causes wives and husbands to regard each other suspiciously, especially if their relationship has been neglected. This neglect is where we need to focus our attention in this lesson.

It is reasonably safe to assume that most marriages began with great dreams and hopes of life fulfillment on the part of both husband and wife. Somewhere along the way love gets lost and isn't even missed. Suddenly the stark loneliness of realizing that you're starving to death for intimacy within the most intimate of relationships becomes reality when you need him and you've forgotten how to reach out.

Middle age is a difficult time for both men and women. A person between the ages of thirty-five and fifty-five or sixty has been portrayed as one trying to walk with children hanging around his neck, on his chest, and parents riding his back. Midlife is a crisis-ridden time. You're standing at the window wondering if your kids will make it on their own and trying to figure out how to make life as pleasant and easy for elderly parents (who may be sick) as possible. There seems to be no space in between the two generations; you're being squeezed in the middle.

Being in the middle is an uncomfortable place to be regardless of age. It feels like you're caught in a trap. It can happen early: the middle child; the peacemaker between battling parents or siblings; or between your children and spouse; your spouse and your parents or in-laws; between clients or members of congregation or staff, etc., and your spouse (would you tell him/her so and so for me) when they are trying to enlist your support; between friends; being too low on the ladder of success in your business for your age; to name only a few.

The feeling of being trapped or held hostage isn't necessarily wanting out of a marriage situation as much as it is just a feeling of being hedged in on all sides and not knowing where to place the blame. The old childhood fear of abandonment, loss of love, and rejection may unexpectedly reappear if there is a forced separation caused by illness of a parent or grown child, or the wife having to stay behind during change of jobs to sell the house—all alone she has to deal with the children and repairmen, prospective buyers, everything that had been shared at least in part before.

It is hard not to get caught and ground to bits in this emotional meat grinder. This is the sort of thing that makes maintaining any type of intimacy in marriage almost impossible because you're too exhausted and wrung out.

Middle age seems to be the time when the body makes changes. The menopause years for some women are extremely frustrating. Changes in hormone balance can affect a woman's whole emotional makeup. She probably doesn't understand herself much of the time.

Men also go through a sort of "change of life" somewhere around forty-nine to fifty-five. It isn't so much metabolism as it is the disturbing realizations of either being at the top professionally and having no more worlds to conquer, or not being where you assumed you'd be professionally at this point, and there seems to be no way to turn. Sometimes, one's position has been usurped by a "razzle-dazzle" young buck who is smart (and knows it) and has a full head of hair and a slim waist.

*Fear of losing his job* (or actually losing it) has caused many men to isolate themselves from family and friends because they feel so inadequate and disappointed in themselves. It is a churning restlessness that eats away at one's very soul. He feels like he is less of a man and very possibly may have temporary impotence, which adds to all the other fears he has to deal with.

Another part of the puzzle is the *specter of the adolescents* who choose this most inopportune time to "act out." Some children sail through the choppy seas of adolescence with very little trauma. No matter how sweet and fine a teenager is, there is always tension during these difficult years. Then there are some teenagers who manage to rock the whole household; there is constant turmoil. Both parents begin to feel like failures. They are falling apart themselves and can't seem to control the children either. Everything they had thought themselves capable of doing is in a state of distress. The very time in life when we thought we'd be able to breathe a little easier has become the most difficult and frustrating. No wonder some people do succumb to the temptation to run away.

*Dealing with alcohol and drug problems at any age is a shattering experience.* It is true that midlife is the time when any tendency to alcohol or drug dependency is likely to increase. It is not unusual for problems and crises encountered during this period to cause one spouse or both to drink heavily or to abuse the use of legitimate prescription medication. This has never proved to be any help to an already bad situation. In fact, this has taken many marriages to the brink of disaster. An alcoholic spouse is terrifying to cope with. Get help early. Don't wait until it is too late. If you cannot get the problem drinker to seek help, you must not ignore your own needs. There are many AL-ANON groups ready to stand with you. Your teenagers will also need ALA-TEEN.

The widespread use of both prescription and nonprescription drugs is causing profound problems in all age groups, ranging from preadolescent through old age. When we began this section, we planned to use it as parents dealing with teenagers. Then we realized that the problem is so much more than only that relationship. One person (whatever age) in the family with a drug or alcohol-related problem creates turmoil for every life he touches. It is a terrible experience for all concerned. Many people seem to think that if they ignore all the suspicions, even the evidence they may have, the situation will go away and they will not have to deal with it. Or they cannot acknowledge that the situation can be happening to a good, church-going, Christian family.

A psychiatrist who works with addictive patients offered a seminar on teenagers and alcohol, marijuana, and other drugs for four Wednesday evenings in conjunction with the usual activities of his church. The first week three couples attended, along with two teenage boys (sons of two of the couples). In the middle of the session, one boy asked his father if he could be excused, was given permission, and never returned. That boy had just been bailed out of jail on drug-possession charges. The next week only one couple showed up and the following week no one came. Now believe me, my friend is not a boring speaker. His facts, case studies, and down-to-earth illustrations will awaken the most easily bored. He decided that people must think that if they don't know the facts, the facts will go away. Reality is difficult to face, especially when it is unpleasant and there are no concrete answers, no guaranteed cures.

Personal experience has led me to believe that facing reality places one in a position of being aware of the many angles of any given situation. So often when the world comes crashing in we say (or someone will say it for us), "Everything will work out. It will be all right." We want to skip over the next part, the process of dealing with the results of the terrible accident, the arrest of your teenager, the divorce proceedings, the incurable illness of your child, or whatever the crisis may be. Walking, stumbling in shock and terror through the tough situations, wondering what the outcome will be, is experiencing the stress that can cause illness in itself.

Bill and I have a very strong feeling that addictive problems need to be highlighted, brought out into the open, and examined from all sides, because we have already lost two generations to drugs alone and there is no sign of the problem diminishing. Institutions can't be built quickly enough to take care of both adult and adolescent addicts. It is impossible for state institutions to give the long-term, controlled environment needed to allow the patient to withdraw and remain free from drugs long enough to overcome at least some of the longer-lasting effects on the brain and personality. Many hospitals report a great increase in polydrug abuse (mixing drugs, including alcohol). As you would expect, this greatly heightens the hazards and increases the difficulty of treatment.

In the late 1960s and early 1970s, marijuana and "hard" drugs were the thing for adolescents to use as a rebellion against parents and the status quo. Gradually, over the years, it has become a middle-class leisure activity, especially marijuana and cocaine. These early users, many of whom were college students, insisted that they were not adversely affected by the use of marijuana. There was no accumulated scientific evidence to show the damaging effects of marijuana on the capacity of the brain to make important decisions, the changes in personality, loss of personal integrity and will power, as well as cellular damage that can now be authenticated. However, we must be aware that no matter how much scientific evidence is produced, it is meaningless unless the individual user of drugs sees what is happening and really wants to change and will seek help. Some Berkeley students were persuaded to stop using marijuana for at least three months, made notes on changes in their attitude and ability to perform in school, and reported that it was as if a fog had been lifted from them and their performance improved amazingly.

One of the frightening things about marijuana is the wide variance in the potency of the drug. Each "smoke" is really an unknown quantity. In 1969 serious research began on the effects of controlled quality marijuana. Based on the findings of these last eleven years, scientists from around the world agree that marijuana is a very dangerous drug. This is not a scientific document, but we want to make you aware of the seriousness of and the risks involved in the use of any drugs, but especially marijuana because it is so available and is "pushed" on children at an ever younger age.

The effects of marijuana are cumulative and dose-related. Alcohol is a very dangerous drug and adversely affects the body. However, physically the body gets rid of the alcohol from one drink in about six hours. Marijuana is stored in the fatty tissues and the THC from one joint (smoke) remains in the body for thirty days. Thus, if a person smokes only once a week, his body is never free of the drug. It continuously acts on him. Smoking five joints a week does more damage to the respiratory passages than smoking six packs of cigarettes. One campus psychiatrist, who in 1956 had a relaxed attitude about the drug, now considers it the most dangerous drug Americans face. Extensive clinical experience has proven more universal psychological effects of marijuana which we will discuss in this section.

Marijuana used even in moderate amounts causes damage to the entire cellular system and because it accumulates in the brain there is irreversible damage to that organ. There are young people in their twenties whose brains show atrophy comparable to that seen in the elderly who suffer from hardening of the arteries and strokes. There is strong evidence that there is great danger of genetic damage or even genetic mutations in marijuana users. Marijuana smoke causes precancerous damage to lung tissues, as well as bronchitis, emphysema, and other respiratory diseases within a year. There is severe mental deterioration, lack of motivation, and symptoms of paranoia.

Several psychiatrists who work with adolescent patients

have characterized the adolescent marijuana smoker this way:

a.  He has changed from an outgoing, interesting person to one who is withdrawn.

b.  His thinking is affected in many ways. Thought formation is distorted. He often doesn't make sense, but feels that he is maturing.

c.  His memory is shortened and his attention span and concentration have been greatly reduced. He may easily forget his own birthdate or events of great significance.

d.  He does not want to be hassled over anything. Merely requesting him to tend to a small housekeeping chore or homework can trigger a major conflict. You can expect him to become angry and possibly even threaten parents or other authority figures who oppose his lifestyle. For some who have a normally short fuse anyway, violence is not unusual toward family members who demand normal participation in life, such as getting up and going to school and observing a reasonable curfew.

e.  Marijuana is a hypnotic drug and the spell is long lasting. This makes it easy for the user to be talked into doing things that normally he wouldn't do. He is very likely to be persuaded to "follow the leader" into the hazardous use of more powerful drugs. The "leader" is always one of his peer group or circle of friends who also smokes marijuana. He unreasonably and shockingly allows himself to be used; is overly generous in compliance to unreasonable demands by friends. This accounts for the stealing of money and valuable items (family treasures) from his family members and when more is needed, he steals from friends and neighbors. The hypnotic effect also explains why it is true that regular marijuana users fall victim to hard drug pushers, extortionists, and other evils. Loss of will power occurs after only about six weeks of moderate use. The user loses interest and joy in activities and studies, or anything that used to be important, including family activities. He becomes aimless and talks about great goals, while doing nothing.

f.  Small amounts of marijuana (about three joints of "street" grade) cause the user loss of memory and sense of timing. His interests become more and more narrowed and eventually he thinks of nothing but the next "high." The chemical stimulation of the pleasure centers of the brain cause the user to become incapable of responding to the natural physical and intellectual stimulation.

g.  There is every likelihood that the marijuana user will exhibit tendencies toward paranoia and/or schizophrenia. This is caused by the chronic disturbances of neural mechanisms which receive sensations. This occurs in people who are psychotic and in marijuana users. This leads to completely inaccurate response to reality. Young users (preadolescent and adolescent) fail to "grow up." Smoking marijuana not only inhibits maturity, but actually causes the user to regress in his psychological development. This is frightening. I observed a counseling situation over a period of time with a particular addict who was hospitalized at age twenty. He was a longtime poly-drug user. At this particular session, which included his parents, he observed that indeed he was making progress; he had actually gotten up on time (without undue coercion), brushed his teeth, and gone to breakfast that morning. To him it was a big deal. I had seen a four-year-old do that and more the day before.

h.  Young users return to an infantile self-absorption and instant gratification. At the time when they should be acquiring the discipline of deferring pleasure (long-term goals), they demand instant pleasure, refusing to learn to cope realistically with the normal emotional storms and problems of the teenage period. They turn to alcohol or marijuana to relieve the tensions of the moment. They do not learn to cope with life and actually ruin their chances of becoming responsible adults.

There are telltale signs of drug use that parents, teachers, and others closely related can observe.

1. A tendency to oversleep and become angry when disturbed. A total disdain for family schedule or getting to school or anywhere on time (or at all) except an activity involving his peer group.
2. A decided change for the worse in school performance, a withdrawal from activities such as sports, and generally disturbed behavior.
3. A change in grooming habits. He may not bathe or even change clothes or brush his teeth without a hassle. It is shocking and embarrassing.
4. Sudden, seemingly unprovoked flares of temper, even to the point of throwing things, kicking the furniture, yanking down drapes, etc. You can expect this to get more violent as he becomes more threatened. It becomes increasingly difficult for him to behave appropriately.
5. A girl may have menstrual difficulties. She may also be involved sexually with her "pusher" and others.
6. Friends who come to your home may change at this point. They are often "weird" looking and possibly sullen. You may feel that you don't belong there any more.
7. There is a certain pallor that defies description in many cases. Red eyes and dark circles under the eyes are common; often the user has a ravenous appetite, especially for candy bars.
8. Watch for needle marks on the arms (are long sleeves always worn now?).
9. Drug users rarely admit that they are in fact smoking pot or using any other drug. You cannot assume honesty at this point, even if he has always been trustworthy.

Older teenagers and young adults, after using marijuana over a period of years, may also use heroin, cocaine, and other drugs. Many mix the marijuana and shill or other drugs with tranquilizers, "uppers," and "downers."

We have spent a lot of space on marijuana because it is a newer problem than alcohol abuse. However, the first drug that the overwhelming majority of youngsters use is beer.

We're not saying this from the perspective of middle-aged tee-totaling Southern Baptists. I was urged to include this by a psychiatrist in one of our local hospitals who specializes in addictive problems. Beer is used widely by very young people because it is easily accessible. You can get drunk on beer just as you can on any other form of alcohol. Beer has become an accepted "good time" beverage. Advertisements show that to be part of the "in" crowd, you really need beer. Eighty percent of high school seniors are beer drinkers. Thirty to forty percent of high school seniors use marijuana and beer. Among the older patients admitted to alcohol drug units, almost fifty percent are poly-drug users, usually alcohol and tranquilizers. There are now a lot of adults on marijuana and they are just as unaccepting of facts and help as teenagers are.

I asked Dr. William Scott, a psychiatrist, some questions concerning addictive problems. Here are some of the questions and paraphrased answers:

**1. Why do youngsters get started using alcohol and drugs?**

A child models after someone he likes and admires. This may be parents or someone important to them. He is likely to develop habits and attitudes similar to his model. If he sees Mom and/or Dad or another person whom he admires drinking beer and other alcoholic beverages, he is not going to understand why it is not good for him also. He can back them into a corner quickly. The same thing is true with smoking. Forty percent of adults smoke (tobacco) in spite of the fact that we have scientific proof that cigarettes are a health hazard. Cigarette smoking is the first step to smoking marijuana. If his model is damaging his health, why should he do otherwise?

Parents must realize that the responsibility of being a model requires discipline, self-control, and perhaps breaking some bad habits of their own. There are cases where children turn in rebellion on their models and assume a peer or older adolescent who is a behavior problem, but is the center of attention. A problem peer group is easier to enter than the group who behaves and studies.

A youngster begins to use alcohol or drugs because of peer pressure, to be one of the gang—and he likes what the drug does. It is an easy way to escape reality and hard work. The sad part is to see the potential of these young people lost. Adult addicts, forty years old, have a better chance to remain free of drugs, but their potential is already so limited. Think of the years that are totally lost to the adolescent addict, and also to their families and the community.

Adopted children have a high rate of addictive problems. Many go through a time of searching (usually at puberty) and wondering who they really are; why they were given away by their natural parents; were they not lovable; did they do something bad; and many other questions. These self-doubts, coming at the time when he is physically rather unattractive because he is growing and developing and all the parts haven't come together, combine to reinforce his poor self-image. He wonders if he really is treated as a natural son or daughter and what it would be like if he were "really theirs." When people decide to adopt a child, they should plan to receive continual family counseling with a child psychologist who is skilled in dealing with adopted children.

## 2. What do I do if I suspect my child is using alcohol and/or marijuana?

If he is a preadolescent, find a child psychologist skilled in addictive problems and get into family counseling without delay. A thirteen- or fourteen-year-old should be taken to ALA-TEEN meetings and the whole family should get into therapy. If he refuses, he should be hospitalized. If he is a teenager, enter him in a hospital with an addictive unit. He must be removed from his environment, be totally free of drugs for at least thirty days so that the residue can get out of the body and he can think clearly enough to cooperate in the treatment. After hospitalization, continued family therapy is very important.

I feel we need to say something to those who may have a **less than perfect family**. Children need to see a united front presented by their parents. If a child is easygoing and even-tempered, it is much easier to maintain a generally calm, pleasant atmosphere. Parents should set the priorities in the home, not the children, but if there is a demanding, manipulative child in the house, it takes sheer determination to avoid great chaos. Children with any sense at all learn very quickly how to play Mother against Daddy. This is devastating and frightening to all concerned. I know how to speak to this problem; I don't know the answers, but we have experienced it. Our older son came into the world with a very complex personality and has continued to be difficult, not only to us as parents but to himself also. Some people seem to have a restlessness and intensity that drives them beyond their ability to cope. Now, I know you're saying, "Doesn't she know about hyperactive children and the help for them?" Yes, I do, and that helps most people; unfortunately it wasn't the answer for us. We began to search for help early and the best we could do was receive counsel and guidance for our own handling of the situation. We learned that loving tough-mindedness and just "hanging in there" was all we could do at times. But we did it *together*. It was crucial to us and to him to present a united front that could not be penetrated by any assault that could come against it. I do not know how people who are not Christians, who do not know the power and strength of prayer, can get through any type of crisis (and everybody has them). All that has kept us sane many times has been the knowledge that our heavenly Father is with us in the midst of difficulty.

In working our way through these years, we have gained in many ways. We learned to depend on the heavenly Father for strength (not just daily, but moment by moment); we really have become a very close family unit; we can identify and understand others who are in painful situations; we learned never to give pat answers; we developed the loving tough-mindedness that I mentioned with the emphasis equally on loving and tough; and we have learned to enjoy and appreciate each other, both our sons, and take life a day at a time, feeling secure in each other and God.

**Moving to a new community is a very stressful time** for the whole family. It is a strain physically, emotionally, and financially. The emotional strain is probably the worst because the move involves exchanging a familiar environment for an unfamiliar one. Family conflict can often be traced to the time of a move. The underlying reasons for the conflict were already there, but the move brought it out. There may be a period of separation if the husband goes ahead and the family stays behind to sell the house or finish the school year. Loneliness in having to deal with life without emotional support is a real problem. Not knowing what your mate is doing or thinking is cause for distress. Planning ahead may eliminate some of the difficulties.

The husband may be enthusiastic about his new job and co-workers, while his wife is having to meet new neighbors, place children in new schools, locate drugstore, doctor, grocery store, etc. It is overwhelming. If the children are teenagers, there is probably some rebellion and resentment on their part. Some teenagers change locations easily, make friends quickly, and are absorbed into the new community with little problem, but a lot of teenagers feel awkward and hesitant about breaking into a new group.

One couple in a sharing group said, "These have been the loneliest months of our lives. Our children are grown and away from home and we moved here (Atlanta) from Chicago away from our family and all our roots. We have each other and we've grown closer, but we've been so lonely. If it hadn't been for the church and Sunday School and the warmth we've felt, we couldn't have made it."

**Illness** frequently occurs during these middle years. This is frightening to the whole family. A heart attack is rather common these days when men, in particular, are so pressured at work, overeat, and underexercise. A heart attack or stroke presents great problems. A disabled father may mean that mother will have to go to work and there will be added duties for older children. A chronically ill mother means she can no longer take care of her family and house. Not only are there the obvious physical problems, but illness can temporarily change a person's personality. Fear and anxiety are the constant companions of the whole family. Somewhere along the way there will also be resentment and anger to be dealt with.

**Death** is a shattering experience. During these years there may be the death of a parent. This can affect the balance of a marriage by triggering subconscious guilt, dependency problems, and just the general pressures of dealing with another emotional situation. Plenty of time should be allowed for the grief process. The open expression of grief will aid the healing process.

**Death of a child** through illness or accident may prove to be a strengthening tie for the parents or it may separate them. Husband and wife have to deal with their grief individually and as a couple. Each needs the support of the other. Perhaps a family counselor or minister will be needed to help restore emotional balance.

When an **aging parent moves in,** new dimensions are created in the family. If one or more parents have to be cared for, some changes will have to be made. There are always exceptions to any rule, but usually people are happier if they are able to be as independent as possible. Some homes run smoothly and everyone benefits by having a "live-in" grandparent. Very often, however, this is a burden on all concerned. Think how difficult it would be to have to revert to living in the home of a married daughter or son. Everyone loses privacy and there are many complications that have to be worked out. Extra demands on an already busy household can only add to the existing tension and frustration. Also, the middle-aged husband or wife may revert to his childhood relationship with the parent. Of course, there may also be guilt about neglecting one's spouse to care for the parent. There must be total openness and honesty about the situation or there will be smoldering problems that will explode into a major fire eventually.

Then the most difficult of all. What if your parent needs nursing care that is not available at home? It is devastating to face the fact that the decision must be made to **have your parent cared for in a nursing home.** The heartache, guilt, and trauma are unbelievable. Only the very wealthy can possibly afford to have the kind of live-in nursing care that is required by so many elderly people. We should be very grateful for excellent facilities for the proper kind of care. However, this is a time of heaping on the guilt. This is also an area that I can speak to with first-hand knowledge. After my father had been very ill for many months and my mother had broken her own health nursing him, he had brain surgery. At the end of his hospitalization he was not well enough to take care of himself; Mother was physically very ill; and we couldn't afford live-in care, so we really had no alternative but to have him cared for in a convalescent center until he regained the strength and ability to take care of himself. He was treated very kindly and the therapy worked wonders and he is home again now. But the trauma, the guilt is beyond understanding unless you have experienced it. I want you to know that you have to be strong enough to do the right thing for all concerned. You cannot allow a parent, a spouse, or child to be torn apart physically and emotionally just because you can't face up to reality and responsibility. You have to do the best you know how to do at the time. This kind of emotional drain will affect your marriage. Talk it out with your mate; be understanding and supportive; help him with logistics; and, above all, express love and affection to the guilt-ridden soul. This could become a time of building family solidarity if grandchildren are around to visit and run errands.

Two other events occur during middle age that are packed with emotion. The **marrying of children** and the **birth of grandchildren.** Becoming a mother-in-law and a father-in-law means you step into a new role. Are you ready? This can be the beginning of a great new relationship or another crisis-loaded situation. Make sure you have cut the cord between you and your married children. Allow them to have the privilege of making their own family patterns, even their own mistakes. Relate to them as adults and try never to be critical or put down your child's spouse.

Grandchildren are usually looked upon as a reward for enduring. Of course, this depends on the attitude of everyone concerned. We have to learn to stand back, not offer too many suggestions. Keep a good perspective on the situation—don't allow a grandchild to become more important than your spouse. Grandparents can have a very special place in the life of a grandchild. Grandparents can be more objective and can do more with a child than the parents sometimes. Our boys have had a very unique relationship with their grandparents. There is a deep bond that was especially helpful during the teen years. Grandparents could say things and be heard that parents could only shout and be ignored. It's a great opportunity if you keep the upper hand.

I asked several middle adult Sunday School departments to participate in a survey asking about problems or barriers to intimacy in their marriage and what they were doing to improve their marriage relationship. Sixty-five women and forty-six men answered the questions. The years of marriage varied from four (a second marriage) all the way up to thirty-eight years. The number of children per family ran from zero to eight; most have two or three. The greatest barrier to intimacy was communication difficulties. This was brought about by busy schedules, demands of children and teenagers, differences in education and values, lack of common interests, financial problems (mentioned only once), fear of being hurt if open and honest, and pressures of family and parents. It was interesting to observe that the men wrote more suggestions for improvement than the women. The men seem more desirous of intimacy, by their answers.

A number of those married over thirty years are desperately trying to get grown children to leave home. There was also stress over agreeing on how to discipline children, and lack of trust in the marital relationship.

This quotation from one of the questionnaires seems to express the stress and desperation of middle age: "I pray that we can hold on until the children realize that we need our time or either when they realize the importance of intimate relationships. We desperately need privacy and time together by ourselves, without the children."

Here are some suggestions this group offered on ways to improve communication and strengthen intimacy:

1.  Put forth extra effort to give my spouse first place in my life. Being together is enjoyable.
2.  Do not allow children to replace your need for relating to each other.
3.  Remember that the greatest thing a father can do for his children is to love their mother, and vice versa.
4.  Be open and generous with love and affection.
5.  Be honest with each other, even when it isn't easy.
6.  Show confidence in each other's ability to cope with problems. Trust my spouse.
7.  Worship together—be a vital part of the church.
8.  Pray together—strengthen our faith and remain aware of God's presence in our lives.
9.  Setting aside special time during the week just for each other—no children.
10. Listen, really listen, to each other.
11. Make time for trips, even short ones together.
12. Try to be more understanding—look at the situation from my spouse's point of view.
13. Let my spouse know how much I love him and that we can do anything together.
14. Show each other the little kindnesses that I'd show to friends.
15. Recognize the need for counseling, either as a couple or family and both be willing to participate.
16. Pray daily for our relationship—our family.

17. Laugh together. Keep a sense of humor. Have fun together.
18. Support the self-esteem of my spouse with gifts of appreciation, concern, and understanding.
19. Bill and I make a special effort not to be separated more than forty-eight hours. There have to be exceptions to this, but it is a good rule to have.

## Work Space

1.  To what degree do you feel you have achieved intimacy with your spouse?
    poor          good          very good          excellent

    Before this course? _____      Now? _____

2.  How has your marriage been neglected?

    How has your marriage been nourished?

3.  Decide now on a plan to strengthen intimacy as a couple this week.

4.  Discuss these problems and offer realistic suggestions. Do you have a similar situation?
    a.  My eighty-year-old father wants to live with us most of the time. When my father and mother visit us, he is very demanding about everything. He decides the mealtimes, lectures everyone about everything, and so forth. We just can't do things his way because he is so demanding.

        Recently, when my mother told my father that they visited with us too much, he flew into a rage, hit and kicked her several times, and broke several things in the house.

        Now my father is planning to come back to see us for another visit and I don't know what to do. He accuses me of being a mean and ungrateful daughter because I won't allow him to live here for good. But I have responsibilities to my own husband and teenage daughter.

        My father tried to commit suicide several years ago,

and he has suggested to me several times recently that he will do it again if he can't come to our house when he wants to. I owe my father more than I can ever repay. He helped us get the loan for our present house and worked hard helping us in the past. I guess I feel guilty in the situation.

b.  My wife and I are in our early forties. We have never had a close relationship during all the years of our marriage. Matters seem to have grown worse since the birth of a son, our second child, about five years ago.

My wife actually seems to avoid any experience which puts us alone. She refuses to go out for an evening or a weekend without the children. I don't even suggest this anymore.

Her coldness is also evident in her feelings about physical affection. She resists intimate contact of any type. When we discuss this, she tells me she doesn't love me after all these years of our marriage. She even questions if she ever did.

I love my wife and I hope we can do something that will help bring us closer together. Where can we start? What can I do? I know I need to be a better husband and father, and I myself am part of the problem.

5.  How can we try to protect our children from alcohol and drugs? Name some specific ways.

6.  What do I do if my spouse has a drug and/or alcohol problem that is getting out of hand? What if we are both drinking too much when under stress? Is this the case?

7.  An executive has suspected that his wife is drinking too much during the day. He is jolted to face reality by a

phone call from the jail where his wife is being booked on drunken driving charges, with other charges pending. While driving the car pool from school, she lost control of the car, hit another car, leaving one child dead and one critically injured. Could this have been avoided? How? What will be the best route for him to take now?

8. A fifteen-year-old girl has gone through extended treatment for drug abuse. She is doing well now and her parents are pleased. Until now they have been very strict and adamant about her not using alcohol or drugs. Now they have relented. She is dating a nineteen-year-old boy who doesn't drink, but she has begged to take a "sip" of beer at parties so she can feel part of the group. They have agreed. What effect might this have? Will it be harmful?

**Case Studies**

Can you recognize yourself or your spouse in any of these? Can you offer any solutions or alternatives?

1.  A government official, married nineteen years, announced to his family that he was leaving home to live with a man. His wife, in a state of disbelief and shock, is having difficulty accepting the situation. Their sexual relationship had been very satisfying (both agreed on this); she had had no clue that this was going on. She says she could handle it better if he had left her for another woman. She is extremely concerned about the effect on their three children. Her life has fallen apart. She and the children will need long-term therapy.

2.  Married fifteen years to a sales representative for a large company, Judy discovers that because of his numerous affairs, she has contracted a venereal disease which does not respond to treatment. They have four children and she elects not to seek a divorce at this time. Because of her anger, hurt, and fear for her health, they have separate bedrooms. They have worked out a truce and the children seem to be functioning well, although they feel the strain and cannot understand the "cold war" situation. One child is beginning to question and feels an unexplained guilt for the unhappiness.

3.  The small town rocked with the news. The pastor and his wife were getting a divorce. It was hard to believe that this could happen to a couple so attractive and so dedicated. A closer look would reveal a problem that had been covered, but left smoldering for nineteen years. During the second year of marriage, while still in seminary, Sue had been depressed after the birth of an unplanned baby. Money was very short, Don's attention even shorter, and though she managed to swap out baby-sitting, Don was always studying or working at the bookstore. Sue discovered during an accidental meeting with

an old boyfriend in a nearby city that she was still attractive and desirable. She had a very brief indiscretion, which she confessed to Don and he forgave her. They made peace and presented a united front to the congregation they served. Sue did all the things that the wife of a pastor should do and was very happy and fulfilled. Then the rumors began to fly. Sue couldn't believe that Don (Mr. Conservative) was guilty of having an affair with one of his counselees, the wife of a Sunday School teacher. Sue was ready to forgive and return things to normal, but neither the church nor Don was ready for that. Don wanted out of the marriage—out of the ministry. He was suffering from a severe case of midlife blahs and succumbed to a lot of feelings that even he was not aware of. Subconsciously, he had always wanted to punish Sue for her early blow to his ego, he was frustrated in his failure to achieve great success and fulfillment in his career, and this was a sure way to have to make a change. Sue will need therapy to overcome her anger, hurt pride, and loss of prestige.

4. Tom was an engineer by profession and an avid sports fan in season and out. Mary had wondered for many years why she had married Tom. They had both been working in a small community, had been thrown together and the people assumed and urged them into marriage. It seemed the thing to do at the time. Mary was an accomplished musician and used her talents in the church choir programs and in civic music activities. Their two children were virtually grown now. Through the years, Tom had agreed that Mary attend concerts with friends, some of whom were male. Mary gradually began to run with a very secular crowd and thought that she had reached the height of sophistication. Just after she and Tom celebrated their twenty-third anniversary, she announced to him that she felt she would be better off socially and musically if they were not married. She needed her freedom to

develop professionally. She expressed surprise that Tom was brokenhearted. Even when she told him how unfaithful she had been, he still wanted to try to make the marriage work. Neither could understand the other. They were complete strangers.

5.  Theresa knew just how to get her parents, Lois and Bob, locked in a fight. Theresa was a fifteen-year-old beauty who was always on the brink of trouble. Theresa was the middle child and only daughter, who adored her father and could get anything from him. She was running around with a wild group of teenagers who were deep into alcohol and drugs. Bob traveled most of the week and was unaware of the severe problems that Lois encountered in dealing with Theresa and her friends. They were literally camping out in the basement play-room (which had its own private entrance) and Lois became increasingly afraid to even go down to check on them. If she tried to enforce the rules of the family, Theresa and friends would ridicule or just ignore her. However, they altered their behavior and spoke to Bob politely on the rare occasions they saw him on the week-ends. Lois was becoming more and more hysterical and could not convince Bob that they had a real problem with Theresa. Fears became reality when there was a drug "bust" with their home as the target. Bob couldn't understand how it could happen; surely there was a mistake. This was only the beginning of the bad scenes to come. Theresa ran away and was gone for several months and when she returned, she was still belligerent, several times being arrested for shoplifting. Each time a heated battle would be fought between the parents as to her participation, whether she should have to face juvenile detention, etc. Lois and Bob began to blame themselves and each other for being poor parents. They have been average church attenders, but it was embarrassing to go now because they assumed everybody knew their trouble and

would look down on them. Bob would not agree to participate in counseling. Finally, Lois and Bob divorced; Theresa moved in with her father for a while and then disappeared again; Lois is still in shock and trying to recover from so many losses: husband, daughter, position, etc.

6. Last week a beautiful young woman in her twenties stayed after the worship service to speak to Bill. She told him that her thirty-five-year-old boyfriend (divorced with child support to pay), an executive in a good company, is addicted to cocaine, and is dealing to supply himself. He had succeeded in making her feel responsible for him. She didn't know what to do. What would you advise? Bill's advice was direct: "Run as fast as you can. Give him the name of this doctor and this hospital and tell him to get the help he needs. You can't make him do it or change him. He has to want to change and get help." She was relieved to get the burden of responsibility for him removed.

# 13. Happily Ever After

*Bible Passages:*          Psalm 23; 32:7; 144:3-4; John 14:1-4

One of the sweetest, most comforting sights in our neighborhood is to see our neighbors across the street go for their daily walk around the block, holding hands. They have been married sixty-two years and are both in their eighties. As I look out my kitchen window and study them I have the feeling that these are two very strong individuals who, even in their "golden years," are a very formidable team. I've watched them from my window for over fifteen years now and have been inspired by their devotion to each other; the little ways they show concern—he works in the yard and she comes out to check on him and they sit together in folding chairs while he catches his breath. It was natural for me to think of them as well as some other wonderful senior adult friends as I began to prepare this lesson. I decided that it can be "happily ever after" if we have maintained the relationship to this point. I asked my neighbors to tell me some things that they thought might help younger couples make it happily ever after.

With a twinkle in his eyes Mr. Key said, "Well, it's still a lot of fun. I guess consideration of each other would be the big thing. Ruth has always been considerate of my needs and desires." She broke in to say, "I thought it was the other way around!" She says that he is a very easy, pleasant person to live with and his sense of humor has brought them through many rough waters.

They were among those who came through the big 1930 Depression and experienced severe financial struggles. This helped make them both aware of financial priorities. Make financial plans early; practice self-discipline.

Mr. and Mrs. Key have always had common interests in community, civic, and church activities. They are favorites at the church among all ages. They continue to have friends among young people; it keeps them young and, let's face it, they are losing their contemporary friends by death.

Mrs. Key had two sayings of her mother's that are appropriate for us today. "If you don't do without the little things today, you'll never have the big things tomorrow"; and "You can't put the same dollar in two places."

Mr. Key's philosophy for everyday living is one we should all adopt: "Every day to make the load a little lighter and the day a little brighter for everyone with whom I come in contact." I can testify that he does this. Our boys always knew that if Dad wasn't available to help fix the bicycle or doctor the injured dog, Mr. Key would come to the rescue. I'm sorry I can't share my neighbors with you.

Bill and I lived in Florida in basically a retirement community for several years and made several observations of senior citizens. The biggest shock of my life was the realization that just because one is a grandparent doesn't mean that he is sweet and kind. When you get older, you just become more of what you were when you were younger. Now that can be pretty bad. A grumpy middle-aged man is going to be a really grumpy old man.

As children grow up and leave home, it is time for the couple to revitalize and deepen the marriage relationship. Increasing, or rediscovering, sharing and closeness is an urgent need at this point in life. Both husband and wife need to have their egos supported. There is also a need to deepen relationships with other couples of various ages. These relationships help replace the loss of children. The spiritual potential of marriage should be further developed now.

If a couple learned to communicate earlier, the passing years will usually increase their intimacy and enjoyment of each other. If their relationship has been a wasteland with little touching, they will likely develop parallel lines with almost no touching. They can live in the same house, but lead very separate lives with little contact.

When the children leave home you can do all the things you wanted to do and never had time or money for. This can be an exciting, adventurous time of life. Be ready to go places, do things, and enjoy each other.

It is important to enjoy each other, but not to overwhelm each other. Husband and wife each need to be secure enough to know that if it becomes necessary, through death, one can live without the other. They both need to know how to care for themselves, their finances, etc., and to develop and lean on their own resources and relationships. Both husband and wife need the support of the other in adjusting to retirement. This is a source of irritation to many couples because schedules are so totally different and old patterns are changed. This adjustment can more quickly be made by couples who have learned flexibility.

For couples who have managed to achieve contentment and intimacy and for those who are willing to continually cultivate intimacy, these later years can be the most fulfilling of marriage.

Bill and I exercise at the athletic center downtown and one of our friends from that activity is an amazing person. George Peterson has been retired from his original career for several years. He was overweight, crippled with arthritis, and had assorted aches and pains. Now he is in great physical condition, looks and feels great. George and his wife, Pat, are enjoying each other and life more than ever. They exercise, travel, play golf, and enjoy being together. One day in the middle of his exercise program, George stopped and went to the phone. In a few minutes he walked by me and said, "I just called Pat and told her I love her. I forgot to tell her this morning. I don't ever want to forget that."

Mr. and Mrs. Charles Knapp have recently moved to Atlanta to be near their children. They are in their eighties and have made a remarkable adjustment to living in a retirement complex in this large city after living all those years in a small south Georgia town. Until a year or so ago Mr. Knapp actively maintained an antique business and was active in all the town's activities. Mrs. Knapp has never been one to sit around and the other day I heard that she is enrolled in a creative writing course at one of our downtown churches. She and a friend ride the bus there and back and have collected even more friends and acquaintances along the way.

Even when the time comes that you need to be cared for in a convalescent facility there is no need to feel that life is over. It is normal that you will feel angry, even if you really know that it's best for you and your family. How you handle your anger will determine how much you see of your family and friends. Make them glad they came. Help brighten the days of those who care for you—the nurses and aides. Be as helpful and considerate as you can of the other patients.

We all assume that we'll never get old or infirm enough to have to be in a convalescent center for the aged. Often the only alternative is death and we do not control that. God is never finished with us till he takes us home to be with him. Let him be incarnate in you until the end.

## Work Space

Ask yourself these questions as you approach retirement, or if you're already there.

1. Do you read a newsmagazine weekly?
2. Do you read a professional interest-related publication regularly?
3. Do you at least scan a newspaper, including the editorial section, daily?
4. Have you attended a continuing education seminar, class, etc., in the past year? If no, have you had an opportunity to do so?
5. What books have you read in the last six months—for recreation? for education?
6. If you teach Sunday School, do you ever vary your approach or do you stick to one style? Do you participate in programs offered to enhance your teaching?
7. What new thing have you learned in the last six months? Have you acquired a new skill? What?
8. Would you like to participate in a continuing education program?
9. Name several areas you would like to explore educationally, recreational or professional.
10. Are you ready to answer God's call to discover and use his gifts?

We urge you to:
1. Make a plan for continuing education. Set your course; do not drift along.

**Seminars/Classes:**
Professional
Recreational
Educational

**Church Related:**
Aids to teaching

Bible study
Soul winning

**Reading:**
Recreational
Professional/Educational
Spiritual

2. Keep a diary—for balance in emotional, business, and spiritual growth.
3. Check credentials of those to whom you listen.
4. Try something new—risk—learn a new thing!
5. Grow and change—only death can stop you.
6. Plan for the future.
7. Plan for retirement.
8. Retire to a good thing, like mission service.

## Review

### Learn to pray and seek God's will

When a person trusts God, he can more easily trust his spouse. Shared religious experience and worship nurtures the whole family. It is important to bring faith and married life together because faith in God brings a transforming power and unity that cannot be experienced otherwise.

1.  Do you maintain a time of personal, private prayer and/or Bible study?
2.  Are you able to talk to your spouse about spiritual, religious matters?
3.  Do you pray for each other? With each other?
4.  Are you both open to God's guidance in your lives?

### Learn to cope with problems and trouble

As Christians, we must not equate prosperity with goodness or adversity with badness. We should use trouble in a positive way for discipline and to strengthen the inner being. This way, trouble will not destroy you, but will polish and refine your life. Life is a continual growth process. Crisis situations are a vital part of that process. Can you help yourself and others in crisis situations? Are you developing resources for coping?

1.  Name some ways you can relate to someone in a crisis situation.
2.  Are you in touch with reality concerning your own family and whatever situation you are involved in or may be facing? Do you know where to seek help? Will you?

### The honeymoon is over (the early years)

How a couple deals with early difficulties greatly affects their marriage in later years. Allowing each other appropriate space and establishing a pattern of togetherness is a vital part of the growing relationship. This is something that must have great flexibility.

Many areas need to be ironed out when the honeymoon

is over. Some are: space, sexual adjustment, handling of money, how to settle differences, adjusting to children, etc. Are you having problems in any of these areas? Write them down. Gently tell each other and talk it out, if possible. Then pray about these areas and your marriage in general together.

## The middle years

Middle age is a difficult time. Midlife is a crisis-ridden time. Fears abound. Careers are on the line and you can pretty well see if you're going to make it to the top. Your children are in a crisis time (adolescence) and your parents may be entering a time of illness or senility. Everything seems to come unglued. We need to give each other the affirmation and support that is desperately needed.

How can you nourish your marriage during these middle years?

Specifically note some areas that need help. Talk about these openly and kindly. Make plans to strengthen intimacy.

## Happily ever after

This is the time to enjoy each other even more than before. Learn some new things. Be adventurous. Be thankful that you have each other. Show and tell your spouse that you love and appreciate him.

# Part V
## Celebrating

# 14. Happy Anniversary

*A*nniversaries and other special occasions give people an opportunity and a reason to look back over the past year, to take time to express appreciation (or sometimes regret), and to determine where you are in your relationship. It is a time for celebration and should not be taken lightly.

There will be times when you'll have to celebrate a day or so early or late because of the day of the week it falls on or for any number of acceptable reasons. But never fail to celebrate and plan ahead for it so you'll both know and be able to make necessary arrangements. Mark off the date or an agreed upon substitute date on your business and social calendar and make reservations for the restaurant and/or hotel and a dependable baby-sitter (if needed).

Use your imaginations for this celebration. You don't have to always go back to the same place. You may need to change the scenery. Some years you'll want to do more than go out to dinner; perhaps you can plan a short trip. It doesn't have to be spectacular, but it will be a special time to get away from everyday pressure and enjoy each other again.

Every day that you are married you are making memories. Learn to change and mature from both the unpleasant and the happy ones. An anniversary is a once-a-year opportunity to reaffirm to your spouse that he is still special, still the most important person in your life and you intend to keep it that way.

Because our anniversary often falls during our summer vacation, we have celebrated in many places around the world. On our twenty-fourth anniversary we were spending some time in the north Georgia mountains. Since we enjoy picnics and exploring the woods, we decided to go up the trail to Rabun Bald (highest point in north Georgia) and find a good picnic spot. Well, we kept going and when we would stop to rest, we would agree that the view would be better a little higher up, so on we'd go. Finally, we had our picnic, but after resting a little we felt that since we'd gone so far, we'd go on to the top. We were both exuberant and proud of ourselves when we climbed the ranger station to view the spectacular mountain terrain. Our sons had camped here often and had described the beauty to us, but even their enthusiasm had not adequately described the feeling that we also experienced of being one with God's creation. It was a beautiful way to celebrate God's greatness and our thankfulness for his having brought us together in his love.

In recent years we have been finishing up a mission meeting somewhere in the world for the Foreign Mission Board. The summer of 1978 we visited mission stations around the world and when we finished we took a couple of days in London to celebrate our twenty-fifth anniversary. Some friends had flowers sent to the hotel which caused the hotel staff to give us special treatment. I needed it by then since I had broken my ankle in Rangoon, Burma, and had hobbled the rest of the way around the world! We were a charming sight as we left the hotel to attend a play: Bill in a summer sport coat (the suitcase with his suit had been lost) and me in a long skirt, tennis shoes, and crutch! But what fun! We'll never forget that anniversary.

Last summer (1979) we were in Cali, Colombia, with six of our single adults, helping with the mission meeting. Bill and I slipped away from the seminary campus to go into town to a hotel for lunch. Actually, it turned out to be a wild taxi ride with a driver who spoke no English (we speak no Spanish) who stopped to pick up a very pregnant lady. Thank goodness we were within a block of the hotel. We had a lovely lunch by the pool and made it back to the seminary safely. Best of all, though, was the slapstick comedy sketch which our six singles performed that evening. They painted a very graphic picture of what the Selfs would be doing twenty-five years from then. There wouldn't be anybody left at our church because they'd all be out doing mission work!

It takes time to make memories and to celebrate, so don't make a hard and fast deadline for getting home. This is the time to be flexible and let it flow. Neither should feel rushed. You'll probably want to use the marriage checkup either before or after your celebration. If you can make time to go over it beforehand, it may provide some areas of discussion. However, don't let the party turn into a grim observance of past sins. Make this a happy, tender time to remember. As you reminisce about the past year, you'll be able to see that you made it through some hard times (perhaps sickness—your own or a child—change of jobs, a move, etc.) and your relationship is stronger than ever. It will ease the fear that many people feel concerning being able to face what the future may hold. Perhaps you learned that difficulty need not be devastating. You'll remember some funny, frantic times, too; like when the baby frightened the cat and the cat ran and climbed the Christmas tree and it came tumbling down just as guests were coming up the steps. Or those awful weeks when both children and husband had the mumps! It's only funny later, looking back.

One couple we know recently had an unusual anniversary celebration. For their twenty-fifth anniversary they went back to her hometown and had a ceremony in the church where they had exchanged their vows the first time. She wore her wedding gown; the minister wrote a special ceremony for them, making it very personal. Their daughters planned the reception and the husband planned a second honeymoon. They are still basking in the glow of that event and are ready for the next twenty-five years.

Anniversaries should help us remember not to take ourselves too seriously. Yes, take the marriage and the commitment seriously, but don't dwell on the pain; learn to see the humorous side of situations. Laughter and good humor will do wonders for good emotional health.

## Marriage Checkup

(Set aside time to go over the two review sections together.)

1. Do you feel that your relationship is superficial or are you growing in your understanding and appreciation of your spouse?

2. Have you improved your communication skills since your last anniversary? If so, how?

3. Express to your spouse your greatest concerns (family, work, etc.). Carefully listen to each other.

4. Have you prayed together recently? If not, why? Can you change this?

5. Have you laughed together recently? Do you have fun? Make plans to correct this if the answer is not a positive yes.

6. Share with each other the happiest, best things that have happened to strengthen your relationship in the past year.

7. This may be a good time to get out your wedding pictures and remember.

8. Have a special prayer time to thank God for bringing the two of you together and ask for guidance for the coming years. Prayer: "Our Father, thank you for bringing us together to love and care for each other. Help us to always keep our eyes and intents centered on you and

your ways. As we stand before thee we want to experience the satisfaction of knowing that we have been open
to your guidance this past year. Thank you for walking
with us through the good and the hard times. As we begin
another year together, let us grow in our love and appreciation for each other. Teach us new depths of understanding, both in our relationship as husband and wife
and also as your children. We pledge anew before you
our love and commitment to each other. In Jesus' name,
Amen."

# 15. 'Tis the Season

Christmas, more than any other time of the year, is family time. It can be a happy joyous celebration, or it can be the loneliest, saddest day of the year.

Your first Christmas together will be interesting to say the least. The blending of two traditions takes skill and the first several years hold the most surprises. Perhaps you grew up always thinking that the tree had to be seven feet tall and in the living room. Your spouse is used to having a small tree in the family room. Her family always had turkey for Christmas dinner; his family always had ham, and on and on. It would be a good idea to talk about Christmas early in the fall. Find out what is really important to each other about family traditions. Take time early to think about what you enjoy most about Christmas. Is it receiving gifts? Shopping for gifts for those you love? Selecting a tree? Decorating the tree and house? Singing carols? Planning and doing something for someone who needs help? The smells of Christmas cooking? Christmas dinner? The parties that usually come with the season? Receiving or sending cards? Participating in the annual Christmas pageant at church? Going to a symphony or a special presentation of Christmas music? Being grateful for all God has done for you? Tell your spouse what the most important part of Christmas is to you. If you have children, make a time to share these things with each other. It is sometimes a surprise to find out what is special to each individual.

Your first Christmas together should be a blending of traditions and the beginning of your own. It is important to remember that when you married you became a new family unit. It's true that Christmas is a family time, but there will come a time when you will not be able to go to the home of either's parents. Also, if your spouse is not made to feel comfortable with your family, or the other way around, be considerate, think of how your spouse will feel and make adjustments. Your first responsibility is to your spouse. Parents and other family members should be understanding and helpful and not create more tensions at this season. Do not allow yourself to be manipulated by a well-meaning parent who says casually, "You will be here for Christmas dinner, won't you? I'm having your favorite dessert." Manipulation on either side is not fair.

If "going home" is absolutely out of the question, get busy and make Christmas special where you are. Yes, you will miss family and friends, but there are so many lonely people who need a celebration.

Traditions are important, but even here we need flexibility. There may be a year when Aunt Sue is too ill to bring her apple pie or Uncle Joe's job as Santa must be filled by someone else. We need to vary our activities and food and other traditions so that the natural changes that occur in families through the years will not be unbearable.

We must never lose sight of why we have Christmas. Read again the second chapter of Luke and rejoice in the birth of Christ. Then remember his death on the cross and his victorious resurrection. We need to keep our celebration from being so costly, so hectic that we forget the worship.

Money can become a real cause for battle at Christmas. One family may have always given lavish gifts at Christmas, while the other family gave more at birthdays. A compromise must be reached. Perhaps meaningful, not necessarily expensive gifts can restore peace. Shop for family and special friends all year long. When you find a lovely china teapot in April that Grandmother would love, go ahead and buy it and save it for Christmas. By the time December 25 arrives, you'll have all your special people taken care of. Making gifts is a very special statement of love. The important thing is to enjoy the gift giving, to enjoy pleasing someone you love. Perhaps the best gift you can give is yourself; for example, an outing once a month for an elderly parent or grandparent or any special time given to someone you love. Decorate your home or apartment and invite someone to celebrate with you, a lonely senior adult, an international student, etc.

Decorating doesn't have to be expensive. Pine boughs, fresh holly, pine cones, or any available greenery tied with a bow make a festive centerpiece or wreath. Lighted candles in strategic places can be a real atmosphere setter. Go to bazaars and Christmas shops in departments to get ideas that you can copy for very little investment.

There are people for whom Christmas and other holidays are very painful. The first Christmas after the death of a loved one is difficult. The loneliness, the feeling of being bereft is almost unbearable. Ministers, counselors, and doctors will verify the escalating numbers of people suffering from depression; suicides and attempted suicides; alcohol or drug crises; and other dramatic manifestations of despair which occur during the holiday season. Many times family members who have any type of emotional or psychological problem choose this special occasion for "acting out." If you know that this may happen it is wise to protect yourself and other family members as much as possible. Invite friends to join you for the occasion. It is much less likely that an unhappy scene will occur if there are outsiders present.

Christmas activities often remind us of unpleasant events that have taken place in years past. If this is the case with you, don't feel guilty about your anxieties, but do something positive to protect yourself. Remember that you are not alone. There are probably more people dealing with heartaches at this season than you could ever imagine. I am having great difficulty as I write this. Next week is Thanksgiving and we enter the rush and confusion of the season which has not been a truly happy time for our family for a number of years. This season has been the high point of emotional crisis situations created by a family member and added to by those in the community who are emotionally disturbed and seeking help from the clergy. The pain of reunions and celebration times when loved ones are absent because of death or unusual circumstances is not easily covered. Let me tell you some of the ways that we have learned to cope with this season, as well as other special family times.

1.  It helps to lift the focus off our personal wounds when we determinedly draw others who do not have family nearby, or who are in town because of the hospitalization of a family member, into some family meal during the season. Our youngest son, Bryan, has already inquired as to the makeup of our Thanksgiving dinner guests, and who will be around our tree Christmas morning. I could give him a few names, but we really never know who will be a part of our extended family. In preparation for this, we buy small trinkets (stocking stuffers) throughout the year and keep a drawer of last minute surprises to avoid a panic. I always plan to cook an extra large turkey or ham and larger than usual casseroles, etc. Allow yourself to be flexible.

2.  Trimming the Christmas tree can be changed from year to year after the children are older, if a change will ease painful memories. Some families have many traditions surrounding trimming the tree and this can be a happy and joyous occasion. Someone always has to do the difficult task of putting the tree in place, untangling the lights, and placing them strategically on the tree. I don't know about you, but we have gremlins in our attic who play in the tree lights all year and no matter how carefully we put them away, they come out having been thoroughly scrambled. Through the years we have had to make adjustments as to when the tree is put up and who is involved. It used to bother me in our early years that Bill was so busy with church members and Sunday School parties that he was too tired to do much with our tree. However, I learned that there's only so much a person can do and, if some years he simply couldn't be available and our schedules couldn't be adjusted, I didn't take it as a personal affront. We made compensations in other areas. As the boys went away to school, we made other

changes. Because of parties and activities we need to have our tree up fairly early and, with no one around to help, I began giving a tree-trimming party. Some years we've had the children of staff members over for supper and to decorate; other years we've had single adults who traveled with us on mission trips. There are many people to whom you could give a special joy by including them in this fun. There's no such thing as an ugly Christmas tree, so don't worry if yours has an unusual personality with so many people participating.

3.  It helps to change the scene of celebration. This isn't always possible, but recently this has helped us. We have a home in the north Georgia mountains where we have another Christmas tree and transport friends who also need a change. Sometimes we have wall-to-wall people, but each senses the needs of the others and we all do a lot of healthy compensating.

4.  Perhaps this should be put first. Before you load up on expensive gifts (and we often think we can dispel despair with things!) make specific plans and set aside money for the special Christmas offering of your church. Then also participate in an activity such as helping to provide Christmas (or Thanksgiving) to a halfway house, home for the elderly, children's ward in a hospital, helping with activities and gifts in an orphanage. See what you can do for prisoners or for a mental health hospital or any other area where special help at this time would be needed. It will lift your spirits as nothing else can.

5.  If you feel yourself becoming unraveled, go and talk it out with a counselor who can help you cope. When we returned from a few days in Florida last week, I noted that I felt like the box of oranges we had sent through as checked baggage on the airplane. When we took it out of the car at home, the cords that had so carefully and tightly held it when we checked it for the trip had been yanked and tugged at so often that it seemed one more try and the cord would break. Then quite possibly the box would

be dropped and all the fruit roll away. Do you ever feel that way? Well, I immediately went to a counselor-friend who let me verbalize my feelings again and offered some succinct suggestions. When your strings have been yanked and tugged at so many times, you need help to cope.

Blended families probably experience the most serious difficulties during the holiday season. Our feeling is that the adults involved (including grandparents) should push their personal feelings and desires to one side and do all that is possible to help the children through this traumatic time. Adults can have an early or late Christmas, but children need to feel loved and wanted and cared for even more at this time. Children should not be made to feel responsible for the happiness of either parent or grandparents, nor should they know that they are the center of a tug-of-war. They will soon learn to turn this to their advantage and then more and deeper problems will arise. Adults are better able to cope with disappointment and pain than children, so make sure that you act in a way that brings security and teaches them the proper way to handle stressful situations.

We've talked about the externals of the holiday season— all the peripheral activities and things that make the season either joyous or sorrowful. Sometimes I'd like to skip over this season and its pain and busyness, but then I remember that without Christmas there would be no ultimate joy, no purpose for living, no reason for the church or missions, no reason for loving and giving.

Christmas is the time when God intervened in history; he came to be with us in the depths of despair and the heights of joy. "And his name shall be called Wonderful, Counselor, The mighty God, The everlasting Father, The Prince of Peace" (Isa. 9:6, KJV). God with us. The celebration of Christmas underscores the depths to which God will go with us. God has become human and when we are in the deepest gloom, we are no longer alone. Perhaps the message we need to receive the most is that when we receive God's unspeakable gift in Christ—God with us—our hopelessness is turned, our despair is understood, our joy is shared. We receive the miracle and then in celebration give the gift of hope and love to others.

## Work Space

1.  Tell each other about your holidays as you grew up. What events stand out in your memory? Remember your favorite Christmas.

2.  Discuss the holiday budget. Be realistic, but allow for a few frivolities.

3.  Where will you be this Thanksgiving; this Christmas?

4.  Make plans so that neither will be too exhausted for the holidays. Don't overextend yourselves financially, emotionally, or physically.

# Bibliography

Achtemier, Elizabeth. *The Committed Marriage*. Philadelphia: Westminister Press, 1976.

Berne, Eric. *Games People Play*. New York: Grove Press, 1964.

Bisagno, John. *Love Is Something You Do*. New York: Harper and Row, 1975.

Chafin, Kenneth. *Is There a Family in the House?* Waco, Texas: Word, 1978.

Chess, Stella, et al. *Your Child Is a Person*. New York: Viking Press, 1965.

Claypool, John. *Stages*. Waco, Texas: Word, 1979.

Clinebell, Charlotte and Howard, Jr. *The Intimate Marriage*. New York: Harper and Row, 1970.

Drakeford, John. *Games Husbands and Wives Play*. Nashville: Broadman Press, 1970.

Duvall, Evelyn M. *Family Development*. New York: J. B. Lippincott, 1957.

Ginott, Haim G. *Between Parent and Child*. New York: Macmillan Books, 1965.

Harris, Thomas. *I'm OK—You're OK*. New York: Harper and Row, 1969.

Herring, Reuben. *Your Family Worship Guidebook*. Nashville: Broadman Press, 1978.

Howe, Reuel L. *The Creative Years*. New York: Seabury Press, 1959.

Hudson, R. Lofton. *Helping Each Other Be Human*. Waco, Texas: Word, 1969.

Hudson, R. Lofton. *Home Is the Place*. Nashville: Broadman, 1967.

Jourard, Sidney M. *The Transparent Self*. Princeton, N.J.: D. Van Nostrand-Rein, 1964.

Knight, James. *For the Love of Money*. Lippincott, 1968.

Leslie, Robert and Alder, Peggy. *Sustaining Intimacy*. Nashville: Abingdon Press, 1978.

Mace, David. *Success in Marriage*. Nashville: Abingdon Press, 1958.

McGinnis, Tom. *Your First Year of Marriage*. New York: Doubleday and Company, 1967.

Penner, Clifford and Joyce. *Sexual Fulfillment in Marriage*. Omaha,

Nebraska: Family Concern, Inc., 1977.

Pinson, William M., Jr. *Families with Purpose*. Nashville: Broadman Press, 1978.

Porterfield, Austin. *Marriage and Family Living as Self-Other Fulfillment*. Philadelphia: F. A. Davis Co., 1962.

Rowatt, Wade. *Marriage: Games or Growth*. Nashville: Convention Press, 1978.

Satir, Virginia. *Peoplemaking*. Palo Alto, California: Science and Behavior, 1975.

Self, William L. and Carolyn Shealy. *Learning to Pray*. Waco, Texas: Word, 1978.

Self, William L. *Survival Kit for the Stranded*. Nashville: Broadman Press, 1975.

Sheehy, Gail. *Passages*. New York: E. P. Dutton, 1976.

Shedd, Charlie W. *Talk to Me*. Doubleday & Co., 1975.

Stapleton, Jean and Bright, Richard. *Equal Marriage*. Nashville: Abingdon, 1976.

Trimble, John Thomas. *Intimacy in Marriage*. Nashville: Broadman Press, 1978.

Tournier, Paul. *To Understand Each Other*. Richmond: John Knox Press, 1967.

Tournier, Paul. *The Meaning of Persons*. Harper and Row, 1957.

Viscott, David. *How to Live with Another Person*. New York: Arbor House, 1976.

Wakefield, Norman. *Building Self-Esteem in the Family*. Elgin, Illinois: David C. Cook, 1977.

Wright, H. Norman. *Communication and Conflict Resolution in Marriage*. Elgin, Illinois: David C. Cook, 1977.

Wood, Fred. *Growing a Life Together*. Nashville: Broadman Press, 1975.